The
Five-Year
Marriage

Shifting the
Marriage Paradigm

ALSO BY ANNMARIE KELLY

Victorious Woman!

Shaping Life's Challenges

into Personal Victories

Victory by Design:

A Mid-Life Woman's Reinvention Guide

to Designing a Life You'll Love to Live

The Five-Year Marriage

Shifting the Marriage Paradigm

Annmarie Kelly

Optimal Living Press

The Five-Year Marriage

This is a work of non-fiction. The events, experiences, and conversations detailed herein are all true and have been faithfully rendered as remembered by the author, to the best of her ability. Some of the names have been changed to protect the privacy of the individuals involved.

To order additional copies and for bulk orders:

Optimal Living Press
985 Old Eagle School Road #502
Wayne, PA 19087
Orders@FiveYearMarriage.com

Library of Congress Control Number: 2017914409
Kelly, Annmarie.
The Five-Year Marriage : Shifting the Marriage Paradigm/ Annmarie Kelly
First Edition.
p.cm.
1. Marriage   2. Married People – Conduct of Life   3. Communication in Marriage
4. Love and Romance.
ISBN: 978-0-9746037-2-8
e-Book ISBN: 978-0-9746037-4-2
306.81
Printed in the United States of America
Cover Design: Dissect Design
10 9 8 7 6 5 4 3 2 1

This book is dedicated

to you, the smart and savvy couple,

who are joining in the grand

Five-Year Marriage experiment

that shifts the marriage paradigm in your favor.

I hope you find pieces of yourselves

sprinkled in the these pages, among

the descriptions and questions and stories,

and that you gather those bits together

and five years by five years,

grow the marriage that is yours and yours alone,

one that honors your SELF, brings you the intimacy you crave,

fills you with joy, and satisfies your soul.

May your Five-Year Marriage be one that your future selves

can celebrate and look back on with profound happiness.

CHEERS!

The Five-Year Marriage
CONTENTS

Introduction

Love doesn't just sit there, like a stone,
it has to be made, like bread;
remade all the time, made new.

Ursula K. Le Guin

For the rest of my life?

Until death do us part?

Those very words kept me from making a marriage commitment. Why?

For years I watched couples take those vows with good intentions and high hopes. Yet, for too many of them, reality turned the "rest of my life" promises into a prison sentence and their "till death" commitment manifested in the crushing of their spirit and the demise of their love. It was sad – and scary.

Then someone, someone I loved, wanted me to say those words and make those promises.

How could I do that? What was I thinking?

I wasn't some teenage kid with stars in her eyes who was looking for the stuff of romance novels. I was a woman who had worked hard to become independent. I had a decent job, owned a house, and I liked my freedom. While I wanted "someone special" in my life, I didn't want it at the expense of my individuality. I also didn't want some open-ended marital agreement with "death" as the end-date.

Do you know what I mean?

Okay, maybe you aren't *just like me*, a "good girl" Catholic with an Italian heritage who grew up in the suburbs of a major city. Instead, you could be a woman who has seen her share of fatherless families with single mothers struggling to support their families alone. Or, you grew up watching one parent dominate the other, and you want no part of *that* kind of marriage. On the other hand, you might be part of the LGBTQ community, and though same-sex marriage is legal in many states, you don't want to do your marriage like everyone else.

No matter what place you're coming from, if you are thinking about marriage, you're looking for some new and improved way to fulfil your marriage commitment. You want to have a marriage that doesn't require losing yourself in the process.

You want to know if there is "something better" for you.

Yes, there is. It's the Five-Year Marriage!

It's new, it's different, and now it's here for you to discover for yourself. The Five-Year Marriage is a marital commitment that does three things:

- Defines how you choose to live your marriage *just* for five years.
- Allows partners to periodically reshuffle the deck in response to change.
- Empowers partners so that each five-year marriage begins with a strong foundation.

The details for creating your Five-Year Marriage, as I developed them over thirty years, are in this book, including:

- Choosing your Five-Year Marriage partner.
- How to get started (The Beginnings).
- What to negotiate (The Nitty Gritty).
- Living your Five-Year Marriage.
- How children are part of the Five-Year Marriage.

In these pages, I also show you how to use those details so you can put together your own Five-Year Marriage contract using a simple form (also included). Along the way I share some of my own Five-Year Marriage experiences, and so does my spouse, Joseph Eagle.

Before you get to all those specifics, first I want you to know how the Five-Year Marriage came about. You might even recognize yourself in some of my story. You see, my ideas about marriage evolved over time.

It was never because I hated marriage. In fact, when I was younger, I *really* wanted to get married. My parents, my friends, and society said it was the right thing to do. When I was a senior in high school, one of the class assignments was to make a "marriage book," which was, I guess, a Catholic version of the visualization collage we now refer to as a "vision book."

In my teens and early twenties, marriage was definitely on the agenda. In fact, I felt as though getting married and having children was my only important goal.

However, years after making that teenage marriage book, I was still single. I wondered if I'd ever meet a guy I wanted to marry, or one who wanted to marry me.

During those years when I was shifting between dating and being single, I started to notice things about marriage. I began to think that "until death do us part" might not be such a good deal for a woman.

Then I met Joseph. He wanted to get married. He asked. I ignored the question. He was persistent. So was I.

That's when I had the idea for the Five-Year Marriage. But it wasn't something we made public. As far as anyone knew, Joseph and I were going to have a traditional marriage.

I remember announcing my engagement. Some people audibly cheered while others breathed a sigh of relief. My mother did both – loudly. She felt that, *finally*, her daughter would no longer be a *puttana* (Italian whore) living in sin, and once I married, she would know what to call Joseph. For some reason, that was a big dilemma for my mother.

Not everyone felt the same. I can still see the grimaces and the pained faces people made when I announced my engagement. Some of the people weren't even close to me or people who knew me well. They were co-workers, colleagues, and acquaintances. It wasn't because they thought I was making a wrong choice. Most of them barely knew Joseph.

The apprehension didn't seem to be about me or Joseph. Rather, it seemed to be about marriage. Many of those people were divorced or living in unhappy marriages. Many sincerely believed that marriage would ruin my happiness.

Even a psychic weighed in with dire warnings about the impending nuptials.

Already feeling apprehensive, what I saw in their faces and heard in their voices frightened me. I quickly understood that more people than I ever realized endured unhappy marriages and living-together-loneliness. Some of those relationships had already ended in divorce, but too many of them hadn't.

All that negativity had me reflecting on the relationships of friends. When I thought about them, I could remember when my girlfriends first met their spouses-to-be. I would get a kick out of those delicious Sunday night calls during which a girlfriend would share the secrets of her Saturday date. Or at work on Monday morning, I'd hear those stories in the teacher's lounge or at the coffee machine. It was fun to see the excited, radiant looks of love on my colleagues' faces.

Living vicariously through their new-love escapades, I often yearned for the same thing. Yes, I wanted someone to love me like they were loved. I was disappointed that it wasn't happening for me. So, when they talked about this or that, *their* stories gave *me* hope that someday it would be me telling those stories.

I'd listen with interest and sometimes even excitement to those bubbling stories of young love from first dates through the engagement. It sounded like so much fun to do tastings with caterers, listen to bands or DJs, try on wedding gowns, and fuss over bridal colors.

I especially loved it when I was part of the wedding party (thirteen times!). I loved being included in the bridal showers, girls' nights out, luncheons and other fun parties. Each time I was honored to be asked, and I cherished my role in many beautiful weddings, even when I had to buy that (usually) ugly and (always) expensive dress that I knew I'd wear only once.

I wanted the same thing.

Yes, I'll admit that some brides were over the top. There was "Bob and I" Diane, and nervous Carol, and oh-so-perfect Nancy. Sometimes their constant love and wedding chatter would become too much. I, like everyone else, would roll my eyes and look at my watch for an excuse to leave the conversation. But those times were few and far between.

For the most part, however, like other family and friends, I listened to the happy wedding chatter. I knew and understood that the brides-to-be were excited and looking forward to what they expected would be *the best day of their lives.*

Unfortunately, for too many of my friends and acquaintances, the wedding and the honeymoon that followed probably *were* their best days. Too often the happy couple didn't stay that way.

Once settled into post-wedding real life, they were faced with normal problems and arguments that come with couples living together. Most of my friends struggled with their finances. Some, because they were still fairly young, had spouses who still wanted to party and go out drinking with the guys. Others had difficult and demanding mothers or in-laws.

In addition, as good Catholic girls, most of them got pregnant way too fast. For a couple of them, pregnancy *was* the reason they got married. For the rest, once they tied the knot, pregnancy was the anticipated next

5

step. If it didn't happen quickly, they became stressed. Mary, for example, confided, "If I could have come off the altar pregnant, I would have been happy." She and her new spouse began trying to have a baby on their wedding night. Mary embraced every old wives' tale, and bought into every pregnancy superstition or belief, from what to eat to a variety of pregnancy-inducing sexual positions. Mary wanted a baby so much that, only a few months after her wedding, when she wasn't pregnant yet, she visited her gynecologist to find out why.

While girls like Mary were working on getting pregnant, and I was living vicariously through other friends' weddings, I wasn't really dating anyone. I seldom went out with anyone more than two or three times. And, when I did date a guy any longer, I'd wonder if he was *"the one."*

That's how it was when I met Jimmy.

It was mid-January, shortly after my twenty-second birthday. He was twenty-seven, in the U.S. Navy, and home for a two-week leave. We spent most of those fourteen days together, and some of it talking about how he was looking forward to being discharged in a few months.

In those first few months we both seemed so ready for a commitment. By the time Jimmy's leave was over, we were "in love" with each other. And, for a while, he *was* Mr. Right.

For the next few months we wrote to each other every week (yes, actual hand-written letters sent through the mail!). When Jimmy came home, it wasn't long before he proposed. I said "yes" without thinking about it twice. That next week, on a sunny summer afternoon, the two of us drove to Philadelphia's Jewelers' Row. We didn't look at too many rings before I found my dream ring. The solitary three-quarter carat diamond was set in a brushed gold band. It fit perfectly, which, according to the jeweler, was a rarity. I took it as a "sign" that we were meant to be. Jimmy bought the ring that day.

As we walked back to the car, and then as we drove down the streets of Philadelphia, we shouted from the car to everyone we passed. It didn't matter if they were walking on the sidewalk, crossing the street, or even just getting into their car. We stopped businesspeople, shoppers – *everybody* – to tell them we were engaged. You would have thought we were the only couple to ever buy a diamond engagement ring. Thinking back on that day makes me laugh and, at the same time, maybe feel a little embarrassed.

Buying the ring was followed by the announcement to family and friends. Then there were congratulation parties, the search for wedding venues and music, shopping trips that helped us fill in the blanks for our life together. We did all the things every wedding-focused couple does.

Looking back, I think we (the engagement and me) were essential first steps in Jimmy's readjustment to civilian life.

One Sunday night in mid-September, Jimmy and I were visiting with Marie and Tom, another engaged couple. The two guys were in the living room talking and watching football while us girls had tea and snacks in the kitchen. I felt like a married lady and I felt good.

Until Monday night…

Marie called and said she had something disturbing to tell me. She said Tom had shared some of the previous night's conversation. Tom was concerned because something in his conversation with Jimmy had Tom wondering if my guy was serious enough and if he was really ready to be married in just six months (our scheduled May wedding date).

At first I wondered if Marie was making a mountain out of a molehill. This many years later I don't remember any of the subject specifics or why Marie's revelation set off warning bells in my head. In fact, I remember wondering if it was true and, if it was, if I should really be concerned. I even thought about not saying anything and just brushing it off.

I didn't.

On Tuesday night I called Jimmy and said I wanted to talk. He picked me up after work on Wednesday. It was a beautiful and warm mid-

September night when we went out for a bite to eat. Over drinks and burgers, I repeated my conversation with Marie. I asked him if what Tom said was true; it was. I expressed my uneasiness with his perspective.

In my heart, I wanted to hear the kinds of things from my fiancé that would put my mind to rest.

I didn't.

When Jimmy took me home that night, as we sat in the driveway of my house, we had one last exchange. I took off my shiny diamond engagement ring and gave it to him. With tears in his eyes, he took it, telling me, "I hope someday I can give this back to you."

In that moment, I wanted the same thing. I wanted to believe that this man, whom I thought I loved enough to marry, really meant it. I wanted to believe he'd grow up and fix whatever that thing was that made him a bad choice for a future mate. And I wanted to believe that we'd be engaged again someday.

That night I cried for a long time. We'd already bought silverware and were looking at pots and pans and dishes and furniture. *I was ready to be a bride.* Suddenly that whole life was snatched away from me.

Ending my engagement wasn't just hard to do. It devastated me. I gained a lot of weight – twenty pounds in a month. I quit my teaching job. For a long time I wallowed in that lonely valley of confusion and depression where many women go when trying to make sense of something sad or nonsensical.

After a couple years, when I emerged from that valley, I was cynical. With new eyes I saw what was happening with too many of my married girlfriends. It seemed like when they changed their names, they changed who they were. They were no longer free-spirited girls. They were traditional wives and mothers.

By the time some of those friends were saddled with babies and bills, they were hinting to me that marriage wasn't all it was cracked up to be. Those once-fun calls about bubbling love had turned into calls that revealed how the perfect guy they married wasn't so perfect. I'd hear things like, "We have nothing in common," and "He comes home and does nothing…I'm exhausted," or "I think he's having an affair."

For too many young marrieds, life wasn't turning out the way they expected. Some became angry or depressed or frustrated. Disillusionment turned into sour attitudes and passive-aggressive behaviors. The once-youthful upward curves of their mouths began to show the first downward bends of bitterness. It was disturbing.

For some, divorce came in the first five to ten years. For others (like those good Catholic girls) they stayed in unhappy marriages; divorce didn't seem to be an option. Some of those women worked really hard to cultivate satisfying lives in spite of their unfortunate union. They naturally poured themselves into taking care of their children. As those children grew up, the women also found jobs, careers, or hobbies, and also groups of friends that soothed and smoothed over feelings of discontent or disappointment.

After a while I started to think that the ones who divorced fared better. They went forward. Most found new spouses, and created happier lives. The ones who didn't divorce endured, but the marriages broke their hearts – and their spirits.

Either way, those relationships became part of the unhappy marriage statistics.

For many years, and for as much as I wanted to have love in my life, I remained wary. So I embarked on a career, bought a house, and was in the process of creating my happiness all by myself. Though I was still open to meeting "Mr. Right," I stopped *expecting* to meet anyone with whom I'd fall in love. So, when I met Joseph, and we fell in love, it was a happy surprise. But, to this day I believe I could have been unattached and had a happy life.

Of course, I'll never know.

Also I think I could have continued simply living with Joseph, without a formal attachment, for a long time, and been happy.

It wasn't to be.

Now, many years later, I don't know what would have happened had I agreed to a traditional marriage. Or if I told Joseph I didn't want to get married, ever. Would Joseph and I have continued as we were? Or would we have broken up so Joseph could meet someone else who *did* want to have a conventional marriage?

I really believe that if we'd gotten married with traditional vows, we would have gotten divorced. It would probably have happened around year seven, when Joseph and I encountered a problem we couldn't fix by ourselves. Joseph agrees.

As it is, we don't have a traditional marriage. We have a partnership that we reevaluate. We take our relationship marriage by marriage. So far we continue to choose the partnership, and each other.

Our Five-Year Marriage has been a stimulating way to live. Joseph and I regularly get to choose, to decide. We always know one or both of us could opt for something else and decide we want to live another way. Some think it's the secret to our success as a couple. *I don't know if that's true*, but having that option may have something to do with why the marriage stays front and center in our relationship. It's not just Joseph and me. It's Joseph, me and the marriage.

That's why, empowered reader, I'm sharing this "grand experiment" with you.

For you and your sweetie, the partnership Five-Year Marriage, might work better for you than a traditional marriage. I can't tell you that it's easier; it's not. In fact, many times I think a Five-Year Marriage is harder. That's because it's based on something scarce in most marriages. The Five-Year Marriage focuses on the partnership with purpose, vision, and goals. It's also about fairness as well as acknowledgement of and mutual respect and appreciation for each other's purpose in life. When those traits become the foundation on which you build everything, it makes a big difference.

Here's what I know for sure about the Five-Year Marriage. It:

- Focuses on marriage preparation over wedding preparation.
- Is a partnership of the most intimate kind.
- Requires a solid focus on your relationship.
- Allows both you and your partner to have the emotional freedom to be who you really are within the relationship.
- Consciously recognizes change. You and I know that change happens, but it's often ignored or rolled into another chapter of your life. In the Five-Year Marriage, you and your partner actively acknowledge and discuss the changes. You aren't a victim, stuck with whatever life throws you. You are empowered and get to choose again.
- Gives your marriage, and the two of you in it, a chance to live a life instead of being boxed into some perpetual corner of discontent waiting for an emotional or spiritual death.

Is the Five-Year Marriage a risk you want to take? Only you can decide.

If you are intrigued and interested in the Five-Year Marriage, here's what to do:

First, read this book so you understand what the Five-Year Marriage is and how to put yours together. That's how you'll get in touch with what you want, what's important to you, and more.

Then, share everything with your prospective partner. Have the conversations suggested in the Five-Year Marriage chapters. Decide what you want for your Five-Year Marriage together.

Finally, create your own Five-Year Marriage contract.

You'll do all that ***before*** the wedding.

After the wedding, as you start living your Five-Year Marriage, if you feel you need more, I have many resources for you at the Five-Year

Marriage website. They include free downloads, seminars, webinars, blog updates, and more. Take a look: FiveYearMarriage.com

If you opt for traditional marriage, I trust you will build a healthy partnership marriage in your own way.

If it helps you to choose, remember that small risks bring small rewards. Big risks bring big rewards. The Five-Year Marriage might be a pretty big risk for you.

If you decide to embrace the "something new" and more challenging Five-Year Marriage, good for you! *You're in for the ride of your life!* I wish you love and luck and a fulfilling life.

Chapter One
Is Marriage Old School?

I think that everyone should get married at least once,
so you can see what a silly, outdated institution it is.
Madonna Ciccone, Singer-Songwriter

Every year more than two million people take that life-changing proverbial "walk down the aisle." The couples, many starry-eyed and filled with love and optimism, take vows to honor and cherish each other "till death." If you ask them why they decided to take "the big step," you're likely to hear something about a "soul mate" and some form of "we're in love."

In reality, the bevy of trite redundancies clash with reality. Don't you ever wonder why, if there is so much love going on in marriage, there are still so many divorces?

According the United States Census Bureau, about 50% of all marriages end in divorce. The average time a marriage lasts is eight years. If you've been married and divorced once, you are more likely to get divorced again. Statistically, the number of marriages that end in divorce are[1]:

41% of first marriages
60% of second marriages
73% of third marriages

The staggeringly disheartening numbers are similar in European countries.

Conversely, a 2010 PEW Research Center report indicates that divorce has been in decline since 1996. That sounds, on the surface, like it could be good news. However, the drop in divorces isn't because couples have found a better way to make marriage work. Unfortunately, the divorce percentages haven't changed.

What *has* changed is the interest in marriage compared to that of fifty years ago. According to the report,[3] in 1960, marriage was the norm and 68% of all twenty-somethings were married. By comparison, in 2008, in the same age group, only 26% were married. After hundreds of years of the same societal standard, that's a huge cultural shift in a very short time! Why?

It seems that, in today's world, many people think the way to avoid divorce is simply not to get married in the first place. As a result, there are fewer divorces because more couples are choosing to just live together.[4] Living-together couples defend their decision by saying that they do not need a piece of paper (the marriage license) with its forced obligations to make their relationship real. They say a legally binding document has absolutely nothing to do with the emotional commitment between two people.

The couples are correct. A marriage license has nothing to do with the heart and soul of a marriage, or with the promises two people make to each other. Many think, as actress Susan Sarandon did when explaining why she didn't marry long-time love, actor Tim Robbins, "If you didn't get married you wouldn't take each other for granted as easily."[5] Sadly, for whatever reason, Sarandon and Robbins are no longer together.

What is even more striking in that PEW report is *why* many couples now prefer living together. According to the report, in 1978, *Time Magazine*, asked registered voters if marriage was obsolete. At that time, just 28% agreed that it was. When that same question was asked in 2009, "nearly four-in-ten survey respondents (39%) say that it is; Those most likely to agree include those who are a part of the phenomenon (62% of cohabiting parents) as well as those most likely to be troubled by it (42% of self-described conservatives)."

Those questioning the "forever" commitment of marriage are making their voices known all over the world. In 2009, Academic and author Helen Goltz wrote a discussion paper about the future of marriage in Australia. She suggested the abolition of marriage licenses and the introduction of short-term contracts.[7]

The Australian government also recognizes the outstanding divorce rate. If an Australian couple is married for less than two years, before applying for a divorce, the couple must – by law - attend counseling[8].

With changing attitudes and negative metrics world-wide, you might wonder: *Does marriage even matter anymore?*

Apparently it still does. Interestingly, the above-mentioned PEW research also reported that "Americans are more upbeat about the future of marriage and family (67% say they are optimistic)." Optimistic about *what*? And *why*? How could so many people think marriage is obsolete and still be upbeat about the future of marriage?

Maybe one reason is that brides and grooms – and brides in particular – still like everything that goes with *getting* married. Though expensive, it's the easiest path because there's a known model for doing it. You can *get* married in a church, synagogue, your backyard, on the beach, or anyplace else. It's the current norm, socially acceptable, and almost always a fun event. In addition, you're the center of attention for a day and people bring you gifts or give you money. It's all part of the "getting" married scenario.

The catch-22 is that, once the partying is over, you have to *be* married. Couples still have to live in the real world, one full of challenges with problems looking for solutions. Most couples are primed for *getting* married, but aren't prepared for the *being* married.

Still, in spite of the dismal statistical predictions for marriage, and in spite of a trend away from marriage, more than half of all people say they want marriage to be part of their lifestyle.

WHY MARRIAGE?
History tells us that the early humans banded together for survival. Mating was essential for the continuation of the species, but marriage wasn't part of it, and neither was monogamy.

15

In their 1978 book, *People of the Lake*, anthropologist Richard Leakey and author Roger Lewin raise questions about the sensibility of marriage as a lifestyle. They theorize that the foundation of marriage, or at least monogamy, might have resulted from a concern about men and their offspring. After all, except in bizarre circumstances, a woman always knows who her children are. It isn't the same for men. Leakey and Lewin conclude that "males have to ensure that they are not being tricked into settling down with a partner who has been fertilized by another male who has since departed."

While Leakey and Lewin's book is almost forty years old, it's not outdated. Women are confident that they are their children's mother but men can never be sure which child they've fathered. You only have to watch a couple of *The Maury Show*'s "Who's the Daddy?" episodes to know what they say is true. Men want to know who their children are. Some will question their paternity because they don't want to be, as Leakey and Lewin put it, "cuckolded" into being responsible for another man's child.

So it seems very possible that, though it wasn't considered marriage as you and I think of it today, the original basis for the union was to ensure a man's paternity. Could marriage be a male-created institution? Very possibly. And, considering how cliché it is to presume that men are more likely to avoid marriage than women, it's ironic.

MARRIAGE AND THE TESTOSTERONE FACTOR
Yes, the testosterone factor. Seriously.

Testosterone is often related to aggression, sports, and athletic ability. It's also part of the mate-seeking experience. Testosterone ramps up to give a man his competitive advantage.

However, in a study done by Peter Gray and colleagues from Harvard University's Department of Anthropology, and reported in *Evolution and Human Behavior*, May 2002,[9] the team drew a correlation between men's testosterone and their marital status. The study found that single men who were looking for love had higher testosterone levels than married or partnered men, who tested with lower testosterone levels.

Through the study, Gray and his colleagues "suggest that lower T levels during the day among fathers may facilitate paternal care in humans by decreasing the likelihood that a father will engage in competitive and/or mating behavior." In other words, when men are bonding with a partner and children, they are biologically more relaxed and comfortable. They don't feel the need to be as aggressive and competitive as they do when "on the prowl" for a mate.

How your body responds to life physically affects your mental, psychological and emotional well-being, right? So, it seems, being coupled is, for maximum health, a man's hormonally preferred state.

MARRIAGE FOR SOCIAL STATUS

Marriage has often been used to promote social status and gain fortunes. While that wasn't particularly unusual in olden days, the American Gilded Age of the late 1800s raised social status marriages practically to an art form. Many of the nouveau riche industrialists, like the Vanderbilt family, had an abundance of money but no social position. They believed that only "a title" would give them that desired social standing.

However, unlike the European aristocracy, the United States didn't have titles that announced one's wealth. Many remedied their dilemma by arranging marriages between their wealthy heiress daughters and European nobles. To ensure a family's importance and prestige, daughters were married off to men who had those coveted titles. Unfortunately those same men often had little or no money.

During that time, parents made the proper arrangements and a young woman was given little choice, *if any*; she was expected to surrender herself for the family's good name and social prominence. The men, young and old, and some good and some not-so-good, needed the money for things like keeping their castles going and their personal pleasures, like gambling and mistresses, humming along. [10]

WOMEN AND MARRIAGE

While paternity and testosterone may figure into martial purpose for men, over time marriage has served many other purposes. Until the twentieth century, when it was unusual for a woman to work outside the home, simple economic survival made marriage a must-do.

If a man wanted to produce legitimate heirs, and a woman wanted a roof over her head, marriage was the practical solution. Love and compatibility often had nothing to do with it.

However, until somewhat recently, in many cultures, women were no more than chattel. A young woman's father arranged her marriage, and there was usually a dowry involved. The dowry was money or property or some valuable asset given to a prospective groom along with the woman. Once an amount was agreed upon, the wedding date was set. Sometimes the young woman didn't even meet the man to whom she was promised until the day of the wedding. Once married, the father's parental authority over his daughter transferred to her new spouse. The woman's job was to have and raise children, keep house, and satisfy her spouse's sexual needs. That was it.

In addition, because a woman didn't actively provide an income, her role in society wasn't given a lot of respect. Until the rise of feminism, when asked what they did, most women would say something like, "I'm just a housewife" with the emphasis on "just."

Until the first wave of feminism challenged the standard, a woman's duty was to be subservient to her husband. Books had titles like *How to Be a Woman* (1954) and *Raise Your Girl to Be a Wife* (1956). Obedience and subservience were admirable traits for women.

If a woman didn't have those characteristics, she was considered headstrong and, consequently, unmarriageable. Many books and plays have been written that purportedly illustrate how empowered women are problem women. Most famously, Shakespeare's *The Taming of the Shrew* (1590) features a man who uses a series of tricks to make his willful bride (the shrew) compliant and obedient. It is considered a romantic comedy and is performed regularly all over the world.

Sadly, that sixteenth century theme showed up in movies in the last century, seemingly one film for each generation. The 1953 film, *Kiss*

Me Kate and 1963's *McClintock* with John Wayne and Maureen O'Hara (during which Wayne spanks O'Hara into submission) are two "shrew" films. 1999's teenage film *10 Things I Hate about You* is a more modern version the same play. *10 Things* also became a television sitcom in 2009.

Whatever the version, the depiction clearly portrays a strong-willed woman as badly-behaved.

In the 1868 novel, *Little Women*, tomboy and free spirit Jo March (alter ego of author and early feminist Louisa May Alcott) wondered if she would be "a literary spinster with a pen for a spouse." Jo married. Alcott did not.

Through most of the twentieth century, and until the second wave of feminism took hold universally, men had almost all the power and permissions in relationships, particularly sexual permissions, without question. "Boys will be boys" explained male sexual behaviors, including what is now called "date rape," but women were expected to be chaste. Passion was left for women who didn't mind being branded with that proverbial scarlet letter.

For more than a century, children sang a playground chant called the K-I-S-S-I-N-G song. It must have been a "teaching song" for young children. If you don't remember it from your childhood, it went like this:

> *(Girl's name)* and *(boy's name)* sitting in a tree
> K-i-s-s-i-n-g! *(spelled out)*
> First comes love,
> Then comes marriage.
> Then comes baby in the baby carriage.

Among families who had "wayward" girls, the "shotgun" wedding was the whispered-about answer to the problem of premarital pregnancy. If a girl got pregnant, she and the baby's father got married, supposedly by force and at the end of a shotgun held by the bride's father. Pregnant Catholic girls weren't allowed to have church weddings. Instead, the sacrament of matrimony was administered by a priest in the tiny sacristy. Perhaps that was to afford the bride a humiliating combination of admonishment and shame.

If there was no quickie wedding, the pregnant girl was sent away to have the baby. Parents often told family and friends that their daughter was "traveling in Europe" or, as it happened in my family, the pregnant girl left home because she was "going away to school to be a flight attendant." After giving birth to a baby put up for adoption, the daughter returned home, as though nothing had happened.[11]

The pressure to be considered a "good girl" was strong, and age didn't matter. In 1957, R. Louis Zalk published a book called *How to Be a Successful Widow*. In his book, Zalk printed a letter from a married daughter about how disgracefully her widowed mother was behaving. Complaining that her forty-seven-year-old mother was dating, drinking, smoking, and staying out all night with men, she asked Zalk what she should do about her "naughty" mother.

In his response, Zalk explained that the younger woman's mother had an illness, specifically, insomnia. The illness was brought on by the "sudden cessation" of sex, which her mother suffered by the death of her father. The remedy? Zalk suggested that the daughter commit her mother to a sanatorium "until she regains her better sense." NOTE: *How to Be a Successful Widow* is still available on Amazon.com because Amazon believes "this work is culturally important."

In addition to strict and biased personal and social codes of behavior, women did not have financial equality. As late as the 1960s and 1970s, if she wasn't married, it was difficult for a woman to get credit in her own name. That included credit for bank cards, store credit cards, car loans, and mortgages. And, without a credit history, it was hard to rent an apartment or turn on utilities. In the United States, it wasn't until 1974's Equal Credit Opportunity Act that creditors could no longer discriminate against credit applicants by gender (or race, religion, ethnicity, etc.).[12]

SEEDS OF CHANGE

Some of the cash-for-titles attitude of those affluent late nineteenth century industrialists carried over into the early twentieth century. But as any Downton Abbey enthusiast knows, social norms began changing after World War I. Women began to develop a sense of personal power. Feminism was barely in its embryo stage, but it was starting to develop.

During World War II, most men joined the military and women took over in the workplace. They held positions at every level in a wide variety of fields, including government, munitions, and aviation. For the first time, women were in charge both at home and at work. The robust role women played in the war effort was depicted in the iconic Rosie the Riveter "We Can Do It" picture. Rosie's button-down blue shirt, red and white bandana, and pumping iron posture was not only a symbol of a modern woman working outside the home, it was also something of a coming out party for the strong woman.[13]

The shift toward a feminist viewpoint began then but was quickly tested after the men came home from war. Though women were in charge at work and home for many years, after the war, women were expected to return to their old ways. Television shows like *The Honeymooners*, *I Love Lucy*, and *The Dick Van Dyke Show* depicted traditional marriage roles for men and women.

The second wave of feminism in the 1970s really shook up the old order. By the beginning of the third wave of feminism in the 1990s, old constructs of male-female behavior were falling away at every turn, including personally, sexually, politically, and financially.

In the twenty-first century world of higher education, an unprecedented number of women earn college degrees. In fact, on most college campuses, women now outnumber men.[14]

In addition, most women work outside the home. While there still isn't gender parity in the workplace, many women have good, well-paying jobs and flourish in their careers. For men and women doing the same job, the income gap is (slowly) closing. No longer are the high-powered, successful women business owners of the mid-twentieth century, like Helena Rubenstein and Elizabeth Arden, considered oddities. Women like OWN's Oprah Winfrey, Spanx creator Sara Blakely, biotech entrepreneur Kiran Muzumdar-Shaw, and OmniMedia CEO Martha Stewart created a blueprint for professional and financial success that thousands of other women model.

In the twenty-first century, women don't need to be married to have a child and don't need to depend on a man for their financial well-being.

A 2013 report from The National Marriage Project at the University of Virginia indicated that 48% of all first births are to unmarried mothers, mostly women in their twenties and many with some college education. In a 2015 article on Cosmopolitan.com, psychologist Joshua Coleman, Ph.D, Co-Chair of the Council on Contemporary Families, affirmed, "Marriage before pregnancy is no longer the only legitimate path."[15]

Unlike the whispered shotgun weddings of previous generations, for the millennial generation, pre-martial pregnancies are celebrated. Instead of being talked about in hushed murmur, they're announced in ceremonies, a practice touted by the rich and famous. The list of unwed celebrity mothers is very long. Actress Mila Kunis talked about her first pregnancy on *The Ellen DeGeneres Show* when announcing her engagement to the baby's father, Ashton Kutcher. *The Today Show* co-anchor Savannah Guthrie announced her impending nuptials on the air, when she was four months pregnant.

In the twenty-first century:
- Men no longer need marriage to have an heir.
- Women no longer need marriage for economic security.
- Women are no longer denigrated for having sex outside of marriage.
- Women can choose to become single mothers without a man being involved.
- Society no longer looks down on divorced women or cohabitating couples.
- There is no longer a punishment for having a love child or being a single mother.

- Women have the opportunity to create their own professional and social status.

The new millennium and its young millennials have changed old norms, haven't they?! Almost all the old reasons for why marriage is important no longer exist.

You have to wonder... if marriage isn't necessary for men or women, and so many men and women even believe it's obsolete, why then are over two million people getting married each year – and that's just in the United States?[16]

What is it about marriage that draws two people into it?

The answer can be as distinctive as the couple making the decision. But some reasons are more or less universal.

WANTING TO BE WANTED
Before women had careers and could support themselves, an unmarried woman was considered an old maid. She was the one who wasn't picked. She was pitied.

Today, the term *old maid* continues to reflect being left out. As the *Urban Dictionary* explains, "an old maid is a kernel of popcorn that did not pop when heated...the ones left behind."

On this count, women and men are alike. Men don't want to be the unpopped kernel any more than women do.

That could explain the plethora of online dating sites.

MARRIAGE AND MATURITY
Marriage is seen by some as an indication of being grown up. It's especially thought of that way for men.

A man in his late twenties or early thirties could easily find he's outgrown the bar scene. Maybe he's outgrown his friends too, or vice versa. Or the guys he once partied with are already married. It's also very possible that he finds that he is meeting younger women (or "kids" as described in a recent conversation between me and two grousing thirty-year-old men) who don't share the same "grown-up" values and interests. He starts looking for something more than having a good time.

Of course, in this twenty-first century, all the same reasons could be said of many women.

MARRIAGE AS SUCCESS

For some, marriage is a goal achieved. For others, marriage is, as sociologist Andrew Cherlin put it, "a way to show family and friends that you have a successful personal life" and it is "like the ultimate merit badge."

In corporate America, some companies prefer executives who are married and are more likely to promote them to higher positions. That is truer for men than for women. [17]

THE BIOLOGICAL CLOCK

As a woman moves past her mid-thirties and inches toward forty, she knows her time for a healthy first pregnancy is getting short.

I DON'T WANT TO BE ALONE

Some marriages happen just because most people don't want to live alone...*or die alone.*

INTIMACY

The one thing that almost all women and men want is intimacy. Sure, you can be *physically intimate* with someone on a first date or a one-night stand. But you can't have *emotional intimacy* with that person.

The only way the closeness and affection of true intimacy can happen between two people is if they trust each other. Trust can only grow in an atmosphere of commitment and continuity.

HAPPILY EVER AFTER
In the idealized version of love, marriage is the natural progression of love. Love is warm and wonderful and gives you a natural high.

In spite of any evidence to the contrary, most of us want to believe that love conquers all. We still want to believe "happily ever after" is possible and being "in love" is enough to make a marriage work.

If you doubt that, spend a day watching The Hallmark Channel. Even when you know it's not reality, you'll still watch a romantic movie and yearn for the sentimentalized happily ever after.

WITH SO MANY REASONS, *WHAT'S WRONG*?
If there are still so many reasons for couples to marry, but marriages aren't lasting, something is clearly off. Given what's been happening in society in the past fifty years, for today's couples, and in its current configuration, marriage is – simply put – old school.

Shouldn't marriage be something more – and better? If it isn't, *why not*?

Could the problem be that people live too long to be married in the traditional way?

HOW LONG *IS* FOREVER?
Was marriage ever supposed to last so long?

In 1900 the average age for marriage was about twenty-five for men and their life expectancy was just over forty-six years old. So, on average, marriages lasted about twenty years. That was long enough to have a few children and raise them into adulthood, which was considered to be late teens. [18]

By 1950, couples were getting married a little earlier, men at twenty-two and women at twenty. The 1950's groom lived to be around sixty-five. The length of the "till death" marriage doubled. Still, if a man and woman stayed together, the marriage didn't have the same longevity then as now.

25

Fast forward to today.

A typical millennial bride and groom, like my recently married friends, Kate and Jeremy, are in their mid-twenties. They can easily expect to live into their eighties, and even living to be one hundred years old isn't a big stretch of the imagination. If Kate and Jeremy stay married to each other, a sixty-year marriage would be fairly normal.

Sixty years!

Almost nothing lasts sixty years any more. Do you know anyone who has a kitchen appliance or home heating system that lasted sixty years? Not likely.

Even well-made houses become outdated in twenty-five or thirty years, often sooner. Unless a house is renovated and refreshed, it's considered obsolete.

Can you imagine keeping your same phone, television, desktop computer, or tablet, for sixty years? Never! Even if those devices are still in workable condition, they need updates.

What about your car? Do you think you could drive it for a hundred thousand miles without needing an oil change? Can you imagine any car that wouldn't need new brakes? And, without regular maintenance, your car's engine would die, the transmission would drop, and your tires would go bald. Every mature car owner knows that updates and regular maintenance are commonplace and recognized as necessary.

If regular maintenance is critically important for a car, doesn't it stand to reason that it's much more necessary for the capricious relationship of two human beings? How can a relationship be expected to keep going and going without the occasional tune-up?

Statistically speaking, it can't. That's why so many relationships don't.

As a result, ideas like the "starter marriage," where a couple considers the first marriage a "test" for future marriages, take hold.

The problem with models like starter marriages is that those are solutions that don't actually change anything. Each marriage partner continues on the basis of old-school, traditional marriage. Those old school ideas are simply no longer valid or working for at least half of the couples in the world.

In 1993, Unity minister Eric Butterworth wrote: "'Till death do us part' has been a rigid commandment. People in a deteriorating marriage have no other resource than to continue with the 'arrangement,' gritting their teeth in an attitude of 'we'll make it work if it kills us.' The sad part is that psychologically and even physically, it often does just that."

Sad commentary, but unfortunately, too true, even today. Year after year, generation after generation, when it comes to marriage, we keep trying to fit a square peg into a round hole.

Society has changed. Economics have changed. Politics have changed. Gender roles have changed. For better or for worse, traditional roles are no longer being played out by most members of society, and particularly not with the millennials.

We, as a society, are evolving. We know that if we want something different or better, we can't keep doing the same old same old things that aren't working and expect a different or better result. Could serious couples be ready for something else? Something that could have a better chance for success?

Yes!

Marriage, as it's been known for generations, is done. Traditional marriage is old school. Old school is out.

It's time for new school: The Five-Year Marriage.

The Five-Year Marriage is the guide to a new way of creating healthy relationships within the context of your marriage. It is short-term, contractual, negotiable and renewable.

The Five-Year Marriage fosters three relationship areas that are important for couples: friendship, partnership, and true intimacy.

The Five-Year Marriage begins with you and your attitudes about marriage and the marriage partnership – new attitudes. Those attitudes come from your beliefs and feelings; they manifest in your behaviors. Behaviors are either the glue that binds two people or the acetone that separates them, marriage or no marriage.

The Five-Year Marriage is for couples, like you, if you:
- Are willing to take a chance on a new way to create the magic that the spirit of marriage promises.
- Understand how the pitfalls of traditional marriage can prevent that spirit from soaring.
- Are willing to make your marriage, and each other, a priority before, during and after the wedding, in your everyday life.
- Have courage.
- Are up for the challenge that demands conscious choice and directed action.

If you agree that traditional marriage is old school and you want something new that could be better and more successful, the Five-Year Marriage could be for you.

Like any marriage, the Five-Year Marriage will be a risk, and a kind of risk that most married couples aren't used to taking. The Five-Year Marriage, as a partnership, will demand more of each of you and more engagement than most couples typically expect.

For your effort, the Five-Year Marriage will give each of you more choice, greater emotional freedom and more real power over your lives. In addition, you will significantly increase the odds of creating a marriage you'll love living.

Your Five-Year Marriage will start now, by talking with your prospective partner about whether you *both* want to have that kind of marriage, and that sort of challenge. You'll see and work at your Five-Year Marriage in a different way from other couples.

So, if you want the illusion of security that traditional marriage offers, you can put this book down now. It won't make sense for you.

If you are still curious, be forewarned: In your Five-Year Marriage, you won't be checking marriage off your list of goals and then moving on to the next thing. Instead, you'll have to really show up in the marriage, *at least 95% of the time.* You won't be able to lip service your way through the challenges of the Five-Year Marriage.

The Five-Year Marriage is one that is distinctive and tailored just for you, with the promise of being better and more successful than traditional marriage. If you think you are the person who is up for the challenge, continue reading.

Chapter One: Joseph's Take

At the end of this chapter, and each chapter, you'll find a "Joseph's Take" section. Since Joseph is my partner in this Five-Year Marriage, I thought it was appropriate to get some of his thoughts and feelings into the mix. He has a very different "voice" than I do and I'm pleased that you can hear some of it. So, after reading what **I'm** *sharing with you, look for* **Joseph's Take** *at the end of each chapter.*

I really like the Five-Year Marriage. I think it makes sense. But, personally, I don't like to talk about having a contract. *Contract* is Annmarie's word, not mine. I like to talk about agreements. I know it's the same thing, but the word matters to me.

If, like me, the "contract" word bothers you, or you don't think "contract" reflects the intention of your relationship, change the word. You can call it your agreement, your sacred pact, your cherished commitment, or another name that gives you both a comfortable feeling. Call your agreement "Harvey" if that makes it better for you.

Whatever you call it, it's an agreement between you and your partner. When you make your agreement, you are doing it with all the significance of a contract. The rest of it can be window dressing. But *the agreement* is the part that is *really* important.

Chapter Two
How About a Watch?

*As I put the wedding gown away, I couldn't help but wonder...
why is it, that we're willing to write our own vows,
but not our own rules?
That's just a little something I'm working on. "*
Carrie Bradshaw, Sex and the City

Change.

It happens. Everyday. Whether you like it or not. Nothing stays the same.

Life changes. People change. Every change is like a stone thrown in the water. It creates ripples of interactions that spread out across your life, often in surprising and interesting ways.

My life changed on the Sunday before Thanksgiving in 1985. That was when Joseph Eagle and I met at a Reiki share in Bryn Mawr, Pennsylvania.

Our first few months together weren't earth-shattering. Though we didn't actually date, we spent a lot of time together. People sometimes asked if Joseph and I were a couple because they couldn't figure us out. However, they seldom got an answer because we didn't *know* the answer. For a long time we just thought of each other as friends.

However, we both felt something was happening between us, though I don't think either one of us called it "love." We thought of ourselves as "hanging out" rather than actually dating or calling ourselves boyfriend and girlfriend.

However, over time, when love did happen, I was glad.

The first time Joseph seriously asked me to marry him was in late 1986. It wasn't something I wanted to do. So, in an effort to avoid saying "yes" or "no", I suggested, "Let's buy a house."

While that might seem daunting to some people, it wasn't for me. I *knew* real estate and I *knew* about houses, including how to get into – and out of – house purchases. I'd been in real estate sales, had a broker's license, and even managed a small office. I'd left sales and management to create the corporate university for a large real estate company in Chester County, Pennsylvania. I was managing that division, which included creating workshops and events that revolved around the various aspects of real estate sales. Also, in addition to the technical knowledge around real estate, I owned an investment property.

With so much background, I had a great comfort level for owning a home. For me, while the house-hunting part was tedious, the sales part was relatively easy. And I knew if it didn't work out, Joseph and I could sell it, split the profit, and go our separate ways. No harm, no foul.

I didn't have that same comfort level with marriage. To me, marriage was "the unknown" and something I wasn't sure I wanted.

So, when I suggested that we buy a house and Joseph agreed, I felt safe.

In early January 1987, Joseph and I told our families. His family was relatively uninterested in the idea of us moving in together, but they were happy for us.

On the other hand, my mother wasn't happy. She was clear about her feelings, but they weren't because of Joseph. She loved Joseph and they got along really well. Actually, Joseph got along with my mother better than I did.

My mother's problem was with *me* not being married. In my middle-class, Italian-Catholic family, that's what "good girls" were *supposed* to do. In fact, as early as my teens, I knew I should get married and have children; I would become "the good wife." Living together wasn't on the "good girl" agenda.

However, in the years before I met Joseph, my broken engagement had changed the direction of my life. From that point on, I saw my future another way. I wanted to be on my own, make my own decisions, and even make my own mistakes. I couldn't do that living with my parents. I needed my own place, my own space.

Of course, I understood that good girls only left their parents' house in a wedding gown, a nun's habit or a coffin.

I chose a different route.

When one of my friends was moving out of a reasonably priced apartment on the second floor of an old house, I decided to rent it. I was nervous, but as fearful as I was, my apprehension was no match for my determination.

When I told my parents I'd signed a lease, my father was furious. He believed I was disgracing him. In retaliation, he stopped talking to me.

My mother's attitude was only slightly better. Because my new apartment wasn't far from a place where she used to work, she seemed comfortable with the location. To my surprise, she agreed to give my prospective apartment the once-over. I thought that was a good omen. Maybe she was coming around…

However, on the day we met the landlord to tour the tiny flat, she viewed the small space with disdain. Then she yelled at my landlord-to-be about her disgust that I was moving from a nice home and "into this dump." Her verbal tongue-lashing made me want to crawl into the woodwork.

Then, the week before I moved, I felt even more behind the proverbial eight ball when my favorite aunt joined my parents in their disapproval. She called me to tell me I wouldn't make it on my own. She assured me that I'd be back with my mother within a month.

In retrospect, I now believe all the family resistance was probably good. It all made me so angry that I remember vowing to myself that I wouldn't go back to the family home no matter what. And I never did.

I moved in early December. My father still wasn't talking to me. In fact, he didn't talk to me for a whole year. My mother wasn't quite as punishing. Still, she was of the "you made your bed, now lie in it" mindset.

Through those first years in my apartment I knew I wasn't just out on my own, I was *all* on my own. I knew that no matter what happened, I wouldn't be able to go to them with problems or for help.

At that time, I was teaching seventh grade in a Catholic school in Drexel Hill, Pennsylvania. I was paid next to nothing and had no benefits. I couldn't buy furniture or much of anything else. I furnished my new apartment with the bed and dresser I'd grown up with and hand-me-downs from a kind cousin and some friends.

Not surprisingly, I struggled. I became a vegetarian, not for health or political reasons but because soybeans, eggs, and cheese were cheaper sources of protein than beef and chicken. For a time, I worked three jobs.

Fortunately for me, most of my friends also had very little money. Instead of going out for dinners or events, we got together at each other's houses for hot tea on cold winter nights, summer hot dogs on the grill, or covered dish dinners for holidays. We were poor but believed it was a temporary experience. We all expected to do better in time.

And we all did.

Because I'd been "the good girl" for so long, living alone and making my own decisions was really good for me. I started to trust myself. I learned that I could handle the challenges that came my way. Knowing that I could make a mess and get myself out of that mess was empowering. I found my independence.

In a few years, I left teaching so I could make more money. I was able to give away the wire-wheel coffee table and oversized, slipcovered chair. I also tossed the bargain-store green carpet, the one that melted if I dropped a match on it. Then I moved to a bigger apartment in a better neighborhood.

In my larger second floor apartment that overlooked the well-manicured lawn of a local elementary school, I felt like I'd won the lottery! I was able to buy a dinette set, a coffee table, and new carpets. I even learned to wallpaper. With my new skill, I jazzed up a bathroom and a hallway.

A couple of years later, I got *another* job with more money and better benefits. I also had a part-time job selling real estate. I bought my first house. I was doing OK.

Remembering those days, I can tell you for sure that those lean years weren't easy. However, with each passing day, I grew more victorious. I developed a strong sense of self and personal freedom that was exhilarating. I wasn't anxious to give any of it up.

Joseph's life experience was almost the opposite.

Joseph grew up in a family with a twin brother and two older sisters. Alcohol was a problem with both parents.

When Joseph was a baby, his father began having an affair. Joseph was eighteen months old when his mother, Rhoda, found out about her spouse's tryst. Long story short, Joseph's father left his family and got a Mexican divorce; Mexican divorces (popular in the 1960s) were easy, quick and cheap, and spouses did not need to be present. Joseph never saw or heard from his father again.

Rhoda, unable to care for her four children alone, got help from her mother and sisters. They stepped in and relocated Joseph's family back to his mother's hometown and into his grandmother's house.

When Rhoda got a job in the next town, she decided to put Joseph's two school-age sisters into an orphanage. For the next several years, Rhoda depended on her family for a place to live as well as childcare for her sons. Rhoda and the boys moved from one house to another, living with whatever relative would take them. They typically stayed with a family until they were asked to leave. A couple of those households included physical and emotional abuse.

When Joseph was six or seven, his mother began a long-term relationship with Vic, an older, never-married, cranky man who was looking for a companion (vs. a spouse). He wanted almost nothing to do with Rhoda's children. Yet, Vic's lack of interest in her children didn't stop Rhoda from accompanying him nightly to one of the local bars.

Meanwhile, Joseph and his brother, Tom, who were both mischievous and high-spirited, were left with relatives. They often got into trouble. The infractions were always small but the boys were well-known in the neighborhood – and with the police. After a while, the local authorities got involved and wanted to put the children in foster care. Fortunately, before the state stepped in, Joseph's grandmother found a place for the boys and their sisters. The school was in Scotland, Pennsylvania, a small town in the central part of the state, about three hours away from the children's home.

The Scotland School for Veteran's Children (SSVC) was a state-funded military-style institution. It was a diverse and multi-cultural environment. The sprawling 185-acre campus provided education plus room and board for children from problem homes. In addition to rows of cottages for young children and a dormitory for the teens, SVCC had a school, gym, library, hospital, chapel, laundry, and several buildings where the students learned woodworking and similar shop skills. Boys and girls were separated and brothers, like Joseph and Tom, seldom saw their sisters.

No one went to SVCC for a "good" reason. Every child who was at SSVC was dealing with the emotional fallout from whatever their strange pre-SSVC upbringing had given them.

When Joseph and his siblings arrived at SSVC, Joseph was introduced to reasonable discipline and responsibilities. Like everyone else at SSVC, he got a decent education but learned virtually no social skills. Still, the school provided him with some sense of home.

For ten years, until he graduated high school, Joseph lived on the rural campus. After graduating, Joseph and his brother attended college at Penn State's main campus. They lived in an apartment, then a fraternity house and, after graduation, got a place together in New Jersey. The two brothers lived together for a short while. When his brother met his soon-to-be spouse, he moved in with her. At that point, Joseph moved back with his mother into her Upper Darby row home, just outside the Philadelphia city limits.

By the time I met Joseph, he had moved out of his mother's house and into an apartment in Drexel Hill, Pennsylvania. He was a case manager at a satellite campus of The Elwyn Institute (now Elwyn), with mentally challenged adults.

While working there, a back problem introduced Joseph to massage. He decided he wanted to be a massage therapist and had a big dream around doing that for a living. He was fortunate to study with storied teachers. He got a part-time job doing massage a couple of nights a week and some Saturdays.

Clearly, we both had challenging backgrounds and diverse needs.

The more we talked about buying a house, the more we realized that it would enable *me* to hang onto the independence *I* needed while giving Joseph the stability and the normal family experience *he* needed. It was a big step but one that made good sense to both of us.

In early 1987, we started looking and, by spring, made an offer on an eighteen-foot-wide stone and brick row house in Drexel Hill, Pennsylvania, a small working-class neighborhood not far from Philadelphia. The house was located about mid-way between both our childhood homes. Built in the late 1940s, it was on a quiet street that backed up to a beautiful historical cemetery. Many of the neighbors were original owners, members of "the greatest generation" who moved into the neighborhood as newlyweds after World War II. Many of those original neighbors had become empty nesters and snowbirds who didn't need the hassle of a house during their winter months in Florida. The neighborhood was starting to turn over to a younger group of owners. It was a good fit for us.

After a little haggling, our offer was accepted. Throughout that summer, Joseph and I scraped together every penny we had for the late September closing.

On the day we moved, we took with us whatever furniture had been in our apartments. We barely filled up a living room, dining room, and one bedroom. However, though we were financially strapped, we were happy and excited and shared a lot of love and dreams. We were among the "young kids" in the neighborhood and we liked it.

Moving was an easier transition for Joseph than for me. While Joseph stressed over having a mortgage, I stressed more over sharing my personal space. Still, for me, living together was a good alternative to getting married.

The following summer, Joseph and I were rounding out our first year of living together. Joseph's August birthday was just a few weeks away and he hadn't said anything about it. I wondered what I could get him for his special day.

I was thinking about that on the night the two of us went for an after-dinner walk. We took our usual trek on the two-mile path inside the cemetery, which was a popular late-afternoon/early evening route for walkers and bike riders. The mid-summer sun was setting and the heat of the day was subsiding.

As we walked and talked, I found a good opening to ask Joseph, "What do you want for your birthday?"

Without hesitation, Joseph said softly, "I want to get married."

I was a little stunned by his answer. And I thought, *Married? Where did that come from? We're living together. We own a house together. Isn't that enough?*

While I was thinking and adjusting to the emotional shock to my system, I wasn't answering. And then Joseph said it again.

"I want to get married," Joseph insisted, this time with a little more definiteness.

I was panicky, and a little annoyed. *What could I say?*

"How about a watch?" I asked. "I'll get you a really nice one."

"I want to get married," Joseph repeated, this time more firmly.

"Hmmm," I replied, still a little stupefied. "Let me think about it."

Conversation over…*for the moment.*

Though I didn't let Joseph know what I was thinking, I wasn't so happy to be in a decision-making state of mind – at least not about marriage.

The way I saw it, marriage wasn't as good for women as all the romance books and mainstream magazines would have them believe. I didn't like how it changed the women I knew. Or maybe "chained" them would be a better description. I didn't want that for myself.

In addition to those outside influences, through the cultural influences of my Italian Catholic family, marriage demanded that women be subservient to men. Getting out from under the thumb of the men in my family – and from any man – had been hard work.

After years of striking out on my own, I loved feeling confident in my ability to stand on my own both personally and financially. The power of financial confidence was just one aspect of my autonomy. Emotional independence was another. I'd reached a point where I knew I'd be happy with or without a man. I wasn't interested in giving that up.

Yet I loved Joseph. My resistance to marriage wasn't about him. It was about the *institution* of marriage. In my mind, the way marriage was done *by everyone* was a setup for failure.

Yes, I admit, *some* people were happy together. But I didn't think that was the majority of married couples. Statistically, almost half of all marriages end in divorce. Even more concerning to me was that I saw a lot of marriages in which the couples *weren't* divorcing, maybe for religious reasons, but they *should have*.

With so much trepidation, I wondered what would happen if I said "no" to marriage. Would Joseph want to break up? Would he move on?

In truth, marriage scared me more than the thought of losing Joseph.

For the next couple weeks I said nothing more about it to Joseph. Instead I rummaged around in my thoughts looking for answers.

First I rationalized. Sure, this was the right time for me. I was a never-married woman who was past the "blushing bride" stage. The man who wanted to marry me was a good man. We were of the same spiritual beliefs. We lived together easily. We had dreams together. We set goals and made plans. It wasn't perfect, but I could see us being together long-term.

Long-term, yes. But for forever? I couldn't see *forever*.

For the next few weeks I walked for miles. I solitarily sorted through my thoughts to find out what I needed to do that would help me release my personal trepidation and discomfort with a traditional idea of marriage.

As I meandered through the streets of my neighborhood, I thought about the many couples I knew who walked down the aisle thinking that they would be together for the rest of their lives. It didn't happen for them. *How could we do it better?*

For as much as I loved Joseph and as hard as I worked at acceptance, part of me kept asking myself, *Am I crazy? How can I even think about give up everything I've worked so hard to achieve?* And, in self-protective mode, I counseled myself, *As of now you have a good relationship with Joseph. Why would you want to ruin it with marriage?*

Finally, on one of those morning hikes, the goddess of logic and creativity joined me. As I let her take over my thoughts, a new model began to form in my head. What if Joseph and I only got married temporarily, for five years? *I could live with that.* Then, *if we still liked each other*, we could get married again.

The more I tossed that idea around in my head, the more I liked it. In my heart, the idea felt freeing. In my soul, I felt at peace. I wondered what Joseph would think. Would he be as comfortable with my odd idea as I was?

One night, as we were having dinner, I told Joseph we needed to talk. The look on his face made me laugh. I think he thought we were going to break up.

He seemed relieved when he found out that "the talk" wasn't about splitting up.

Instead, I shared my "Five-Year Marriage" idea. At first he thought I was kidding. I assured him I was not.

"We'll get married for five years," I proposed, "and if we still like each other at the end of five years, we'll get married again." I also explained that I believed it was the only way I could comfortably and optimistically marry anyone.

Once he knew I was serious, Joseph and I talked about some basic logistics. After playing around with the idea in his head, he agreed to create this new model for marriage with me. We agreed to marry – *but just for five years.*

A couple weeks later, for Joseph's birthday, we invited our mothers and siblings to celebrate Joseph's special day. We welcomed our guests and served up beer and wine and some snacks. Then we all sang "Happy Birthday" and watched Joseph blow out the candles atop a homemade chocolate cake. While everyone was enjoying dishes of cake and ice cream, we announced our plans to marry. We didn't have any money for a ring. Instead, we used my father's wedding ring (gifted to me by my mother) as my engagement ring. Joseph presented it to me in the midst of our surprised family members.

After we told our families, we began telling our friends and coworkers. When we told everyone the date was only six weeks later, I know a couple people thought I was pregnant. That still makes me laugh.

One of my friends, Jane, offered the beautiful backyard of her home in West Chester, Pennsylvania, for the ceremony. We tried to find a church, but without a strong affiliation with one, we were having a hard time. We took Jane up on the offer.

The summer of 1988 was exceptionally hot. Still, almost nightly, Joseph and I walked around our cemetery-park. We talked about what we wanted our wedding ceremony, and our life together, to be. For a while we focused on feelings, like how we wanted our marriage to feel. Then we shared our hopes and dreams for the next five years. From those conversations we came up with some goals and plans. Once we had those details in place, our conversation centered on our ceremony. We decided on a made-to-order ecumenical-style ceremony with a few wedding rituals.

As the Labor Day weekend rolled around, we started putting our ideas on paper (and I worked on finding a wedding dress). Our wedding ceremony became a conglomeration of various religious and spiritual wedding traditions. By mid-September, the ceremony became our own.

The week before the wedding, Joseph bought a new suit. And, after much trial and tribulation, I finally found a dress – in the JCPenney catalog.

On September 24th, 1988, Joseph and I were married in West Chester, Pennsylvania.

At the request of our hosts, Jane and Lou, and because of their concerns about space and parking, we limited the number of guests to twenty. Because neither Joseph nor I had ever been married before, we felt obligated to invite our immediate families. Unfortunately, between our six siblings, our best man, the minister, and their families, we reached that "twenty guests" limit pretty quickly. As a result, we had almost no other family or friends present. Joseph and I had to tell too many of the people we cared about that they couldn't be at our wedding. It was the one blemish on our special day. Other than that, it was just the kind of wedding we wanted.

As far as anyone could tell, our wedding day was fairly traditional. Joseph and I didn't share our Five-Year Marriage decision with too many people. At that time, it was a good decision!

Whenever we shared our unusual marriage idea, some people laughed and didn't take us seriously. Some others reacted with disdain. They hated the idea of the Five-Year Marriage and felt that Joseph and I were debasing the institution of marriage. *I never understood that attitude* considering how many people marry with almost no thought past the wedding ceremony.

Still, when I explained the logic of the Five-Year Marriage, most people were intrigued; most were also a little concerned. They wanted to know if we were going to get a legal marriage license (we did). But, I would tell them, people who live together will typically say that they don't need a piece of paper to prove their love. Along that same vein, we explained that we didn't want a piece of paper to get in the way of our five-year commitment. Once they understood, many of those curious people were supportive and told us that would be interested to see how it was going to turn out.

Joseph and I felt like we were embarking on an experiment. But, actually, it wasn't just a feeling. *That was exactly what we were doing.*

In addition to our unusual Five-Year Marriage, I bucked tradition by not changing my name. That, too, was often treated with derision. One woman at my office perfectly summarized the expressions of others when she laughed and said: "Oh, you're doing *that* dumb thing."

However, then, and even now, I question why women change their name at all. Not changing my name wasn't just because we were only getting married for five years. I liked (and still like) my very long Italian last name, as well as my much-shorter business name. So I kept it.

Once the wedding was over, life returned to normal. During that first five years, the marriage met typical expectations. We were newlyweds and probably had the same up and down experiences that most newlyweds have. But, overall, it was a good chapter in our lives.

At the end of five years, Joseph and I were married in the Williamsburg Chapel in Arlington Cemetery near our Drexel Hill, Pennsylvania, home. The minister was from the Science of Mind church. I invited three girlfriends with whom I was friendly at the time. Afterward, we drove to Pennsylvania's Pocono Mountains for a weekend honeymoon.

While that first marriage was mostly happy, I wouldn't say the same about the second marriage. Halfway through that marriage we did what many young couples do. We hit a "wall" in our communication. That is, something bad happened between us. It was emotionally damaging. We couldn't figure out a way to fix what had happened. No matter how we tried to right that ship, nothing changed. The problem developed into a solid wedge between us.

After many loud arguments, slammed doors, and tears, I told Joseph that if we didn't fix the problem, it was going to be our undoing. I told him the only other way I could think of to deal with the problem was to get outside help through marriage counseling.

Though I'd been to therapy before, Joseph hadn't. He was nervous that a therapist would "open up a can of worms." At the same time, he knew we weren't fixing the problem ourselves, so he agreed that getting the insight of a third party might be the only way.

Marriage counseling wasn't easy, or inexpensive, but it was a positive experience. Joseph and I both learned a lot about ourselves. While we learned a lot about the inner workings of our relationship, I think what we discovered about ourselves was more telling and more useful. Also, Joseph later said that, because he was so afraid to go for treatment, if it wasn't for the Five-Year Marriage, he probably wouldn't *ever* have gone for therapy. I don't think our marriage would have lasted otherwise.

It was during that second marriage that our five-year commitment took on real significance. During that relationship, and as a result of counseling, we started to put together the constructs that we've been using through several marriages. The work we did in counseling took us into the re-contracting period for our next marriage. Using the tools we put together during that difficult period, we figured out what to affirm, tweak, or change in our relationship. It was a challenging process of growth.

That year, 1998, we bought another house. It was new construction and wasn't finished on time. As a result, we spent the summer in a small twin home in Lansdowne, Pennsylvania. It belonged to friends who had moved to a new home and were waiting for their now-vacant old house to sell. We were grateful for the short-term rental but it was without air conditioning. As a result, we spent most of our evening hours that summer at the local coffee shop or nearby book store talking about our future, our next five years.

The process we began that year, including the content, timing, and venue, became known as the "Family Meetings." We continue those Family Meetings to this day, though sometimes we are more regular and diligent about having them than at other times.

Also, since then, most of our marriage planning starts three to four months in advance of our new marriage. Except for Five-Year Marriage#6. In 2013, Joseph and I started earlier because so much had changed for us between 2008 and 2013. Some of that change was just normal life. However, much of it was because, instead of focusing on our own plans, both our mothers needed our attention. I used to say Joseph and I had "moms-in-stereo" because we were their primary caregivers. It seemed, during those years, that if we weren't doing something for one of them, we were doing it for the other one. Both of our mothers passed away on February 10, one in 2010 and the other in 2012. Freaky, huh?

Most people agree that there is something striking about the death of your last parent. For Joseph and me, it was a reminder that we weren't getting any younger.

So, after many discussions about unfinished business, next chapters, and legacies, in February of 2013, we began our marriage re-contracting conversations. The process wasn't simple or pretty, and knowing (like it or not) retirement was someplace on the horizon didn't make it easier. Deciding on whether there would be a next marriage, and if there *was* to be one, what would it look like, was a long and tedious process. That August, on vacation in Town Hill, Maine, and while hiking in Acadia National Park, we made a final decision to go again.

As challenging as the process of re-contracting is, one of the fun things about the Five-Year Marriage is that each time we decide to continue together, we celebrate with a small wedding.

Later that year, the wedding ceremony for Five-Year Marriage#6 was performed by Pattie Painter, one of the women I met doing Victorious Woman interviews, and who is featured in my book, *Victorious Woman! Shaping Life's Challenges into Personal Victories*. She brought her spouse, Tom. We invited my cousins, Maryann and Richard. Joseph's best man, Danny, had passed away a few years earlier; we were happy to have his widow, Pat, join us and bring Danny's energy with her. We also invited Joseph's brother and sister-in-law. However, they were not able to attend.

It was mid-afternoon when Joseph and I exchanged our vows in a beautiful ceremony in a quiet outdoor alcove at the Tyler Arboretum in Media, Pennsylvania. To my surprise and delight, Pattie included the poem "Love" by Roy Croft. Hearing the title tickled a long-buried memory. In my mid-teens, the poem was a personal favorite and one that I believed, in my teenage mind, was perfect for a wedding. But, as an adult, I had long forgotten it. The memory sent chills up my spine and, frankly, the words were more appropriate at this wedding than they would have been at earlier weddings. Having that poem included in the wedding ceremony was a special treat!

That day, under a beautiful blue sky, amid the foliage of the arboretum's bountiful trees, bushes, and flowers, and with a few butterflies adding to the beauty around us, Joseph and I spoke new wedding vows. We could feel the warmth of the September sun and the love of everyone around us. It was sweet, and we were happy.

As of this writing, our weddings have included the already mentioned Wedding#1 in West Chester, Pennsylvania, Wedding#2 in Drexel Hill, Pennsylvania, and Wedding#6 in Media, Pennsylvania.

Wedding#3 was in 1998. It was the year we moved. Our temporary housing situation lasted until just a couple weeks before our wedding date. Those weeks were filled with packing, unpacking, and many adjustments, including learning to find our way around our new neighborhood. That year I'd gotten tickets to be part of the Conan O'Brien television audience. Instead of having a wedding, we drove to New York City for the weekend. I always think of 1998 as the year we got "the Conan O'Brien blessing."

Wedding#4, in 2003, was performed during a lunchtime mass celebrated by Father Jude Michael Krill, OFM, at my alma mater, Neumann University. We shared the Mass with some of the Sisters of St. Francis and employees at the school. Father Jude blessed us with a Prayer of St. Francis, customized for us, and the sisters extended their hands in blessing. It was very special. In fact, that wedding is still Joseph's favorite.

In 2008, Wedding#5 was supposed to be at Washington Memorial Chapel in Valley Forge, Pennsylvania, a national memorial dedicated to George Washington and an active Episcopal Church. However, a couple of weeks before our wedding, the minister suspended the weekly service at the chapel to take care of a pressing family matter. That seeming setback didn't stop Joseph and me from going to the chapel anyway. We took with us the "wedding box" that contained our original wedding ceremony, wedding vows, pictures, and some other memorabilia.

It was raining on that late September day. The weather worked to our advantage. The usually crowded and busy Valley Forge Park was almost empty, and we had the beautiful Gothic Revival chapel all to ourselves. As we sat in an almost century-old pew, just the two of us,

Joseph and I repeated the words we had vowed to each other at our first wedding.

One of the interesting blessings of that day was unexpected. During our private celebration in the chapel, we only saw one person. It was a man who was putting up a flag for a weekend service. He was around just long enough to greet us, chat briefly, and take our picture. It's the only picture we have of that wedding.

After living the Five-Year Marriage for more than twenty-five years, here's what I know:

- Marriage is the hardest thing I've ever done. Marriage and the friendship and intimacy Joseph and I share are part of the partnership fostered by the Five-Year Marriage. It's the most interesting and rewarding thing I've ever experienced.

- Joseph and I don't have a perfect marriage. Like every marriage, it's a work in progress with ups and downs. Joseph and I came from contrasting backgrounds, but each one was very challenging in its own way. Working through the squabbles created by those dissimilarities alone was and is an ongoing test of our love and commitment.

  In addition, through the years, we have had more than our share of financial problems, including the kind that came from both Joseph and I starting businesses within six months of each other (they are our children). We also had a tenant who lived in my investment property who decided not to pay rent. He got away with it for eighteen months. It wiped out any savings we had.

  More recently, as the primary caregivers for our mothers, we also served as power of attorneys and executors for our mothers' estates.

  In other words, we don't have a charmed life. We have the same kind of distractions and challenges most people have. It's our Five-Year Marriage that keeps us focused on each other, and brings us back when we get off course.

- Like everyone else, we're flawed people. Those flaws often show up in our relationship. But, and I repeat this often, no one is perfect. The Five-Year Marriage, complete with regular reality checks, helps us keep things on track.

- The difference between our marriage, as a Five-Year Marriage, and a traditional marriage, is that Joseph and I acknowledge the flaws and make a conscious commitment to work with them in the context of the marriage.

- The Five-Year Marriage Joseph and I created is still evolving. *We're* still evolving. New problems come up. New people come into our lives and bring about new situations. Sometimes those situations enhance our relationship and other times they challenge it – and challenge us – as partners.

- The Five-Year Marriage is the one thing that keeps us on track, keeps our relationship focused on what's important to us and helps us keep moving forward toward a common goal. It creates the bond that is our life together.

Will we continue together? I don't know.

At this point in our lives, we have fewer things taking us off track, fewer financial distractions, and fewer family obligations. We also have more reasons to stay together.

As the same time, old challenges are still present and new ones keep popping up.

With that in mind, Joseph and I plan for the future, but we don't take it for granted. We don't expect that we'll be together until we're dead. We expect we'll be together for this marriage.

Personally, I think I'm a better person because of my relationship with Joseph. I believe he feels the same way.

Whatever happens going forward, the Five-Year Marriage has been a good plan for us. I can honestly say we've had a good run and I'm glad we did our marriage this way. Yes, it was, and still is, a risk. Yes, it wasn't, and still isn't, the easiest kind of marriage commitment.

However, it's what Joseph and I chose.

If you are thinking about marriage, I believe the Five-Year Marriage is a good way to do it. However, it is really only for you if you want a partnership-style relationship. Not everyone does. Some people marry for things that the Five-Year Marriage wouldn't be designed to cover, like status, power, or emotional security – or, at least, the illusion of that kind of security.

If you still aren't sure if a Five-Year Marriage is what you want, the next chapter may help you make up your mind.

Chapter Two: Joseph's Take

When Annmarie first suggested that we only get married for five years, I was surprised and taken aback. I had a lot of questions:

- What do you mean that you only want to get married for only five years?
- What happens after five years if you don't want to stay married to me?
- Is this an easy way out?
- Why *five* years? Is that a long enough time to really get know someone that you are living with?
- Why not *ten* years instead?

All of these thoughts and questions kept swirling around in my mind. I wasn't sure what Annmarie was up to and if this five-year idea was a bad deal for me.

But once Annmarie explained the purpose and reasons why she suggested being married for only five years, I was on board with it. Now I really can see that being married isn't a "life sentence" but allows us to grow as individuals and that makes the marriage grow.

The Five-Year Marriage isn't the easiest way to be married, but I'm glad we did it this way.

By the way, at the moment we've had six marriages...*and I still don't have a watch*!

Chapter Three
Five-Year Marriage Basics:
The Five-Year Marriage Partner

The great marriages are partnerships.
It can't be a great marriage without being a partnership.
Dame Helen Mirren, Actress

In late 2016, actor Rob Lowe was a guest on *The Rachel Ray Show*. She asked him about the success of his twenty-five-year marriage. He thought for a second before saying, "Somebody asked Alfred Hitchcock what makes a movie great and he said it's all casting…and I think marriage is the same way. It's *who* you *choose*."[19]

Rob Lowe is onto something. Much like Alfred Hitchcock said about the casting of a movie, your Five-Year Marriage will rest on you and your partner, that is, "who you choose." While you can fix this and change that, what you need for the Five-Year Marriage is the kind of "casting" that sticks. If you aren't the right partners, the marriage just doesn't make it.

This chapter will help you get into a 'casting' kind of mindset.

So *what kind of person* would want a Five-Year Marriage?"

It's a question that seems to imply that someone who isn't willing to enter into a traditional marriage, with its lifetime commitment, must not be serious.

I disagree. I think a better question is: what kind of person *wouldn't* want a Five-Year Marriage?

Knowing the answer to *that* question could be the difference between happy and miserable.

Yet, except in some very odd cases, there's really no way to delve into the mind and heart of a prospective marriage partner.

53

Or is there?

Yes, you can scour their Facebook, Instagram, or Twitter feeds, and you can run a background check. Those sources will give you some information. Still, unless there are seriously offensive pictures or comments, or s/he committed a crime, how much will you really learn?

Yes, there are classes a couple can take. Some couples *do* go for pre-marital counseling, including the kind offered through some religions. While those classes have good information, they require a couple's focused participation *and* follow-through. Most of the people I know who have gone to classes like Pre-Cana, Pre-Marriage or Engaged Encounter did so because it was required by their religion. The couples admit to varying degrees of interest and participation. However, they concede that they mostly sat through the classes and waited for them to be over.

Clearly, planning a life together is not as much fun as planning a wedding. It's hard work without much immediate gratification.

The average couple uses approximately 250 hours to plan a wedding and a honeymoon. There are books and websites that tell couples what to do. Directories are filled with wedding planners, wedding designers, and wedding coordinators. Each has a function in the style, shape, and logistics of your wedding. They give you what you want (within your budget), handle the stressful aspects so you don't have to, and do whatever you need to make everything happen seamlessly. They are the people who create the wedding day of your dreams.

After the wedding, the wedding planners get paid. Then they move on to the next bride and groom. *Then what do you do?*

Where are the actual *marriage* planners? There really aren't any.

Maybe that's why most couples focus on the wedding but they allot little or no time to thinking about what happens afterward. Yes, of course, there is cursory consideration to things like where the couple will live, having children, dealing with in-laws, and maybe there's even some pre-marital talk about money. But that's about it; not much else is discussed, and certainly nothing too substantive.

Think about how odd that is. After all, we know a wedding is over in a day. Couples spend thousands hiring someone to help with that *one* day.

Incongruously, we expect marriage to last a lifetime and couples presume they can navigate marriage's rough waters on their own. *Isn't that a strange imbalance?*

And, in spite of that, there is still a belief in the "happily ever after" fairytale. If pre-marital or newlywed problems arise, couples embrace the "we love each other and it'll be fine" rationale. Reality challenges that adage. The statistics prove that love alone isn't enough.

If you are choosing to be a Five-Year Marriage couple, you need to do more that plan a beautiful wedding. You need to think outside the box, starting with figuring out whether or not you and your prospective partner are good candidates for a Five-Year Marriage.

Who *is* the right kind of partner for a Five-Year Marriage?

At its core, the Five-Year Marriage puts the greatest emphasis on the *partnership* aspect in a couple's relationship. While the Five-Year Marriage isn't a business, there *are* similarities. How can businesses succeed if the partners aren't compatible? They can't, and they don't. Partnerships, whether it's in life or in business, need companionable and well-matched partners to make it work.

Some balk at the idea of making marriage sound like a business. Many suggest that looking at marriage as a business will kill the romance. Well, okay, yes, *it could*, if romance is the *only* reason two people are together. But it isn't, *right?*

Romance, and the accompanying physical attraction, is a time-honored reason why couples get together at the beginning. It's the reason for having sex and could play a big part in helping you get that proverbial groove back. However, romance is *not* the *main* reason for marriage.

What *is* the reason? It's a good question, with many answers. Here are two typical reasons:

- Money. There are some financial benefits to marriage: couples save money when buying for two, married men get better jobs, health care can be cheaper (especially if the company allows dependents on a company plan).
- Children. When parents are married, their children benefit by having more opportunities in life. Many couples see marriage as the only right way to provide those children with the benefits and opportunities of the stable environment of a two-parent family. And, based on some research, they could be correct.[20]

Though neither reason is romantic, both are solid motivations for marriage.[21]

So if you're one of those who doesn't think it's romantic to treat marriage as a business, understand this: there's no romance in divorce either. I can't think of a single divorced person who won't attest to that fact!

As a Five-Year Marriage couple, it's in your best interests to see your Five-Year Marriage as two business people starting an organization or new venture. Think of yourselves as entrepreneurial and innovative. Good partners create successful enterprises.

It's not too different in marriage. Marriage, as a partnership, is the most important and challenging venture of your lives.

When understanding that the foundation of marriage is partnership, it's reasonable to presume that some people are better suited to partnerships than others. The key to success with your Five-Year Marriage partner is that you are both reading off the same script. That is, while you may have separate personal goals, you agree to have the same joint goals. You don't agree on one thing together and then each of you has some unsaid goal or agenda for yourself. That's something that works against your Five-Year Marriage.

For example, if you decide you aren't going to have children for five years, one person can't decide independently to stop using birth control after only two years. The spouse who does that isn't honoring the couple's own agreement.

Or, if you decide you're going to save money to buy a house or new car, you both have to be able to stick to the plan and not sidestep by spending thousands of that earmarked money on a big screen TV.

One of the benefits of the Five-Year Marriage is that you are both checking in with each other regularly. From the beginning you know that *at least* every four to five years you will be reviewing, assessing, and rethinking where you are and where you want to go together. If you get off track, you will be able to get yourselves going in the same direction (or choose not to).

MUST-HAVES: THE SOLID SEVEN

Is your partner a Five-Year Partner?

While you can do all kinds of tests and assessments to find out, here are seven behaviors that can give you "fast feedback" on any prospective mate, even in the earlier days of dating. These seven "must haves" are self-reporting gauges to use as your relationship evolves:

Emotional Chemistry
Ongoing Dialogue
Dependability
Personal Responsibility
Freedom
Fairness
Mutual Respect

Emotional Chemistry
Whether it's a marriage or a business partnership, good chemistry between the two people is a must. However, there are numerous kinds of chemistry. Some of the same components of business chemistry are the same as the components of emotional chemistry – and some aren't.

57

Emotional chemistry is a powerful attraction. It's that special feeling you have with another person when you know the two of you are on the same wavelength. It's an inexplicable *something* that happens between you. If someone asks you what's so special you might say, "I can't explain it but we just *click*."

Emotional chemistry isn't that same thing as that "butterflies in my stomach" romantic chemistry everyone loves to experience. It's also not the smoldering sexual magnetism that makes you "hot" just thinking about your mate. Though both of those are important, especially in the beginning "attraction" stage of dating, neither one is enough for a long-term connection. Ask any couple who had *only* great romantic chemistry or *only* amazing sexual chemistry early in their relationship. Most of those couples can tell you that one or both of them expected wedded bliss because they had such "great chemistry." However, when the butterflies flew away and the heat wore off, they were left with a lot of living-together-loneliness.

For the Five-Year Marriage couple, the chemistry that's most important is emotional chemistry. It doesn't mean that you agree on everything. *You won't.*

It also doesn't presume that where there is romantic and/or sexual chemistry, emotional chemistry naturally follows. *It doesn't.* Why not?

Emotional chemistry doesn't mean you and your partner are soul mates. *You could be* – or not.

Emotional Chemistry also doesn't mean you are virtual mirror images of each other. *You aren't.*

However, what you will have is have that "special connection" two people have when they "click" with each other. As Dr. Craig Malkin, a clinical psychologist at Harvard Medical School, explained in a Match.com article, "You must have some basic physical attraction for there to be any chemistry at all. But something else also happens with the way people respond to and complement one other, and the way they've learned to interact in their relationships. When two individual's styles fit — i.e., when they create *psychological synergy* — that's when you have chemistry."[22]

How do you know you have the psychological synergy that leads to emotional chemistry? That can be tricky.

No matter how much you think you're alike when you're dating, you must face a stark reality: You and your prospective mate come from two separate worlds. Even when things like religion and culture are the same, you two were brought up in distinct families. Each family has its own version of the world, including a view of relationships. You have house rules and rituals that are unique to the family you were raised in. You're accustomed to those ways of organization, prioritizing, problem solving, and everything else.

That one fact alone is probably the biggest challenge to emotional chemistry. Yet, as important as it is, that detail is also usually ignored, overlooked, or dismissed by almost everyone.

In addition, your own experiences, and your reactions to those experiences *from before you two met*, are singularly yours. They've caused you to think in unique ways about the stuff of life. For instance, maybe you had a parent, sibling, friend, or past lover who was controlling, so you balk at anything that seems overprotective or domineering. Or you enjoy particularly good encounters with people of a certain political perspective or ideology, so you gravitate to those with similar views. On the other hand, if in the past, you felt that expressing your true thoughts and opinions resulted in reproach or an argument, you believe it's best to avoid conversations with those with whom you disagree.

Through those types of experiences, you've formed opinions and patterns of thinking or created useful behaviors all designed to make you feel safe. Up until now, those patterns, thoughts, and behaviors have worked fine.

However, life has quite the sense of humor. You are very likely to be attracted to someone who is not the same. An introvert can easily be attracted to an extrovert. A conservative might find someone with a liberal viewpoint to be fascinating, or vice versa. Or the two of you might feel the same, but in an ironic twist, your future in-laws go out of their way to do the very things that challenge your long-standing internal "feel safe" patterns. The movie *Meet the Fockers* is a hilarious depiction of exactly that problem. Greg Focker's parents are go-with-the-flow kinds of people. Fiancé Pam's parents, particularly Pam's father, Jack, are the polar opposite. Even though Greg and Pam seem to be perfectly matched in values, temperament, goals, and life, Pam's father has unique ways of creating unending challenges for Greg's personal sense of security.

That'll happen.

When you're thinking about entering a Five-Year Marriage, how you two, as a couple and as partners, handle the resulting clashes brought on by your differences will either strengthen or chip away at your marital partnership.

Emotional chemistry is complicated but here are a few ways to think about it:

- The two of you are different, but when it comes to your values, you are in sync.
- You see your relationship as bigger than you two individually. Together you are the creation of a whole that is greater than the sum of its parts. That is, you are good on your own, but when you work together, you both move further faster.
- Your differences seem to complement each other. For example, you're always serious and s/he lives on "the lighter side."
- When you are together, something shifts inside and, even without anything being said, you feel oddly soothed or at ease.
- When something happens in your life, good or bad, s/he is the first person you think about telling.
- You feel like you can turn to your partner when things aren't going well and you know you will get his/her support.
- S/he is the one person who can help you shift out of a bad mood.
- You both feel you want more for each other than you want for yourself

One of the first things I noticed fairly early in my relationship with Joseph, when we took our first vacation, was that we got more done together. I'm a great planner, but Joseph is better at sticking to a schedule. So, even though I might have made a plan, if he wasn't moving things along, we might not have seen as many things as I really wanted to see. I also noticed it when planning to buy our first house and also when starting businesses. We didn't always agree, and one of us seemed to take turns taking the lead in a project, but whatever we did, we got more done together. I even noticed that was true when the process wasn't easy or comfortable for one or both of us, like when I lost my job shortly after our wedding.

At the same time, I struggled with the fear of losing the freedom of my individual identity – my SELF. It was a really big fear for me, but not something that (I think) even crossed Joseph's mind. I'm not sure if it was a male/female issue or not. But it was important to me that he understood my need and supported it. Most of the time, he did and did it easily.

*Still, what we found out from those experiences was this: To keep the essence of our Five-Year Marriage we had to work at growing together and becoming **inter**dependent. That wasn't easy for either one of us. However, our emotional chemistry made our budding Five-Year Marriage experience seem easier and more doable.*

Wouldn't it be awesome if emotional chemistry could be bottled? Unfortunately, it can't. It can't be manufactured, either. You really have to pay attention to whether you two have it or not.

Personally, for as much as is demanded of both of you in the Five-Year Marriage, do you think *not* having emotional chemistry is a deal-breaker?

Ongoing Dialogue
When the two of you are talking, does one of you do all the talking and the other one is simply nodding and agreeing? That's not two-way talk.

Understandably, at the beginning, there's often an infatuation period where you really want to please each other and may hold back sharing some strong opinions or feelings. Sometimes the early stages of a relationship bring on some shyness about conversation or about disagreeing. Also, at the very beginning, it feels like everything the other person says is great, and you want to agree with everything s/he says.

While that behavior isn't terribly unusual during the first few dates, it can't be a continuing conversational pattern. After you have those initial get-togethers out of the way, and especially if you are already engaging in sexual activity, the two of you need to be having two-way talk.

If one of you prefers to keep things to himself or herself, that's not going to work for the partnership demands of a Five-Year Marriage. The "woman of mystery" and the "strong silent type" of guy can be interesting and good for fun. But neither one makes for a very good partner in a Five-Year Marriage.

One thing to consider is that one partner may be more verbal and is more likely than the other to start a dialogue. Also, one partner may be faster at communicating than the other; many people need time to think about their response. That's not a problem in of itself.

However, when that conversation is started, the ability of each of you to communicate effectively and your willingness to speak up on your own behalf is crucial. Specifically, it means that you are in touch with what you want, are able to freely articulate it and, as will happen, you are able to disagree with your partner without feeling like you'll be muzzled. It's worth noting that not everyone can talk about something "on cue" and may need time to think before talking about a serious matter. That's fine, as long as you (1) make a date to talk about it and (2) aren't using time as an excuse for procrastination or avoidance.

Also, in the Five-Year Marriage, there's no place for "yes men" or "pushover women" (or vice versa) who simply give lip service to an idea or promise without a serious thought to the meaning or responsibilities of the agreement.

How can you get into a partnership with someone who can't or doesn't want to have an ongoing dialogue about what's important to you or to your mutual relationship?

You might be able to get away with that in a traditional marriage, but it won't work for a Five-Year Marriage.

When it comes to ongoing dialogue, what do you notice about who talks the most, who shares the most, and how easy (or not easy) it is having a conversation? The answers to those and other communication-related questions matter.

Dependability
Dependability means you're there for your partner. That means you do what you say you're going to do. You're reliable. Dependability isn't a euphemism for something else. It's a tangible and noticeable expression of your ability to support your partner.

Dependability is physical and emotional. Both show up in small everyday ways.

On the physical side, dependability means having a steady job and a decent FICO score. It also means that if you say you're going to call or text or pick your partner up at a certain time, you do it. If you agree to make the restaurant reservations, you make them. If you're the one who is looking up some couple-related information, you have that info ready the next time the two of you talk about it. You pay your bills on time and, when you notice you need it, you pick up the bread and milk on your way home from work.

What about emotional dependability? In the 2014 movie *That Awkward Moment*, Jason thinks his new girlfriend, Ellie, is perfect for him. However, when Ellie's father dies, Jason doesn't go to the funeral. Later, Jason goes to Ellie's house and tries to minimize his bad behavior. Ellie is cold, and Jason seems confused. Before walking away from Jason, Ellie explains, "Being there for someone when they need you, that's all relationships are."

63

Well, in the real world, being there for someone isn't *all* relationships are. However, it *is* a *crucial* part of your core connection. After all, lots of people can be around when things are running smoothly. You're the one s/he needs when they aren't. If you can't be there, why should s/he bother with the relationship? If s/he can get more help, empathy, support, and responsiveness from co-workers, family, and even the clerk at the local convenience store, you are unnecessary.

Emotional dependability also involves a feeling of security about how your partner feels about you and your relationship. Is your courtship an emotional roller coaster? Does s/he love you to death today and is blissfully happy, but tomorrow s/he pulls the rug out from under you (e.g., by saying s/he doesn't know if s/he is ready for a serious relationship, marriage, or parenting)? Then, all of a sudden, you wonder where you stand, and you're confused or stressed about your future.

Or, you both agree to something. Afterward s/he exhibits some passive-aggressive behavior, like being cranky and short tempered. Or s/he engages in another behavior that includes withdrawing or withholding or some other version of "the silent treatment."

What if you just can't be sure of your partner? What if you have to ask a million times, or s/he leaves you hanging, and you're waiting or wondering if s/he is going to come through for you?

If it happens only once, that *might* be a bad day. If it happens more than once, if it's a *pattern of behavior*, it's not healthy. In time it will become toxic, maybe even abusive.

That's a deal-breaker for the Five-Year Marriage.

In the Five-Year Marriage, you make conscious agreements about your life together. If you are going to decide on something with your partner, you need to be confident that both of you will go in the direction you agreed on or will have a good reason for changing course.

Dependability dovetails into trustworthiness. The latter can have many meanings. *What does it mean to you?*

The dictionary says that *trustworthiness* means "able to be relied on as honest or truthful." Do you make a distinction between dependability and trustworthiness? If you do, and aren't specific with each other about that difference, you're sure to experience a clash of values or expectations. When that happens, you and your partner need to quickly have a conversation about the two qualities, what both mean, and why one or both are important to you.

If you are choosing a Five-Year Marriage, look for dependability. When you notice a lack of dependability (you'll see it first in the little things), *pay attention*. If your partner can't be dependable in the small ways, s/he won't be dependable in the big ones either. Cut your losses and move on. It's easier to end a relationship sooner than later, and definitely before your future is influenced by your partner's dependability, *or lack of it*.

What's important to you about dependability and how does your prospective partner show you s/he is dependable?

Personal Responsibility
Do you each take responsibility for what's happened in your life – the good, the bad, and the ugly? If not, why not?

Yes, bad things happen to good people. Life isn't fair, and sometimes you get the short end of the stick. But when something doesn't go as well as planned, it's necessary to figure out what you could have done better in that situation to prevent it from happening again. Not every failure, career setback, or personal disappointment that happens in anyone's life is because of someone else.

That's what Annie failed to realize in the movie *Bridesmaids*. Annie's best friend is the bride, Lillian. Annie is jealous of Lillian's relationship with another bridesmaid, Helen. Throughout most of the movie, Annie blames every problem in her life on Helen, from losing her job to wrecking her car and having man troubles. However, throughout most of the *Bridesmaids* story, Annie fails to realize that her own behaviors are the real source of her problems.

Like Annie, many people are guilty of playing the blame game. Also like Annie, many of those people are simply failing to take personal responsibility for their own lives.

So if, in *every* story, your prospective partner tells you how all the bad things are always someone else's fault – a family member, a co-worker, or just someone else – it won't be long before everything that is wrong in your relationship is *your* fault. If s/he didn't get a promotion s/he deserved because the boss doesn't like him/her, *that's a real possibility*. It happens.

However if it's *somebody else's fault* that s/he didn't get the promotion *and* it's *somebody else's fault* that s/he was late to an important meeting *and* it's *somebody else's fault* that s/he was in a fender bender on the way home from work, that's not a bad week; that's a pattern of behavior.

The reason this is so important to a marriage, and *especially* for the Five-Year Marriage, is that everything either *won't* go right, or won't go your way, all the time. In fact, you can count on facing challenges related to those two events *at least* 25% of the time. When that happens, both of you need to figure out – together – what went wrong. Then you decide how to fix it – together.

If you get to the end of a Five-Year Marriage and one of you blames the other one for everything that went wrong, there's no reason to stay in a relationship with that person. If one of you is never responsible for any of the problems or missteps, you don't have much of a partnership, do you?

One role of the Five-Year Marriage is to acknowledge problems. Both of you will be responsible for some things separately. One of you might always be late, and one of you might not be great at listening. Those are both individual problems, but ones you can work on together.

Of course, like couples in every relationship, each of you will make a mistake from time to time. Neither you nor your partner is perfect. Sometimes one of you won't feel like accepting responsibility for what went wrong. It happens. When it does, you need to discuss what

66

happened with each other and reach an understanding. Something has to change, or it isn't fair to either of you.

When a lack of personal responsibility is consistent, when it's a *pattern* of behavior, that's when it's a problem. ***It's the patterns that matter.***

In the Five-Year Marriage, you choose the goals and behaviors that work for you and your marriage partnership. You also acknowledge what works and what doesn't work. When it doesn't, *together*, you *each* need to take responsibility and decide if and how you can improve going forward.

How well does your partner accept personal responsibility? How well do *you*?

Freedom

Freedom in the Five-Year Marriage means being free to be your SELF, that is, who you really are, in your essence, while respecting the relationship.

In each Five-Year Marriage, many things will change – life happens, children come, careers evolve, friends leave, people die.

Each shift out of what you are used to and into something new changes you and changes your relationship.

The "trick" is to allow your SELF to evolve organically and let your Five-Year Marriage develop with it. Admittedly, it's no small feat. However, in the Five-Year Marriage, you are forging a type of communication that should enable you to maintain your SELF more easily than couples in traditional marriages.

How do you make that happen?

Here's one example: Maybe you and your family or you and your buddies rent a cabin every fall to go hunting. Or you and your girlfriends or sisters take a trip every year. Whichever one of you does it, maybe that event makes your partner crazy. What do you do?

If one of your SELF things isn't hurting your partner or your family, you should be able to continue doing it. However, if chipping in on the cabin or taking that girlfriend trip is financially damaging to the family, that's different. You don't necessarily have to give it all up, but you may need to rethink the frequency. For example, he can go hunting with the guys every *other* year and she and her girlfriends can travel someplace *closer* and less expensive.

Are there SELF- fulfilling practices or traditions that you feel your partner is taking away from you? Are there ones you want your partner to change…and is making that request being unfair to your partner's SELF?

Fairness
Fairness shows up in many ways. Also, fairness can differ by situation or circumstance. Like many of the other Five-Year Marriage partner traits, it's important to be in agreement about what fairness means to each partner. I often say fairness is being "even" so that one partner doesn't get too much more (attention, consideration, etc.) than the other.

The *best* definition of fairness, as it relates to the Five-Year Marriage, comes from the Merriam-Webster dictionary: *fairness* is "marked by impartiality and honesty: free from self-interest, prejudice, or favoritism."

The *sweetest and most sensible* way I've ever heard fairness explained was by an older man, recently widowed. He and his spouse had great emotional chemistry and were happily and lovingly married for a very long time. When asked what the secret of marital happiness was, he talked about how he and his spouse shared and believed in each other's goals and dreams. His weren't more important than hers, and hers weren't more important than his. Because of that, he explained, "We wanted more for each other than we wanted for ourselves." As a result, they each helped the other work toward their dreams. That's fair.

Of course, sometimes one person needs more of something than the other. That *will* happen from time to time. But it can't happen *all* the time and in *every* situation.

When you make your partner's needs and interests a priority, you are more likely to make decisions that are fair for both of you. That fosters trust, respect, and a host of other traits that result in true intimacy. Fairness rules!

How hard do you two work to keep things fair between you?

Mutual Respect

Mutual respect is a definite prerequisite for any marriage. It is, however, critically important for the Five-Year Marriage. You need to clearly define mutual respect for yourself. Then, with your partner, decide what mutual respect means to the two of you.

Some typical expressions of mutual respect include:

- Valuing each other's opinion.
- Listening to what your spouse has to say, even when you don't agree.
- Checking with each other before making major decisions.
- Taking interest in each other's work and interests.
- Not insulting or intentionally embarrassing your spouse in public.
- Honoring your partner's input and opinion.
- Avoiding interrupting when the other partner is talking.

Mutual respect acknowledges that you have differences and similarities. More importantly, while you don't always have to like the differences, you accept them. When you disagree, and if and when you argue, mutual respect means you are willing to listen to the other side. When partners demonstrate mutual respect, each one treats the partner as well as s/he treats other people – and hopefully better!

Basketball Hall of Famer and former United States Senator Bill Bradley said it best. He described mutual respect this way: "Respect your fellow human being, treat them fairly, disagree with them honestly, enjoy their friendship, explore your thoughts about one another candidly, work together for a common goal and help one another achieve it. No destructive lies. No ridiculous fears. No debilitating anger."

Of course, people being people, mutual respect can easily get lost in the hustle and bustle of everyday living. If allowed, mutual respect can die and partners will start treating the barista at the local café better than their spouse. That's not how it should be. Ever.

On a scale of one to ten, where do you score yourselves for mutual respect?

The *Five-Year Marriage Solid Seven* qualities are a good foundation for a partner in *any* relationship, but are *essential* for a partner in a Five-Year Marriage. When noticing if and how your partner demonstrates these "must have" traits, you can more easily determine if the sweetie you've been dating has what it takes to be a Five-Year Partner with you.

Does it seem like too much? Honestly, it *can* feel like it's a little fussy to pay attention to each of these. When you're first dating, and especially when you feel some heat with someone, you aren't likely to want to bother. Also, some things won't come up for the first few months. You may be so excited to be together that you may not notice if there is true "ongoing dialogue," and your "freedom" doesn't seem so important. Still, start noticing when your partner is being dependable (or not) and if s/he accepts "personal responsibility" when something goes awry (or not).

Then, as the relationship starts shifting from "new" to "established," you need to start paying conscious attention to all the "must-have" traits. Yes, it takes time, a lot of it. Prepping for a Five-Year Marriage takes probably as much time as planning the average wedding. But remember: the wedding is over in a day. Poof. Done.

Don't you want your marriage to last five years? And, at the end of it, don't you want to still like your partner enough to get married again? That kind of relationship doesn't happen by accident.

Also, if you have a partnership like that, the rewards are big ones. You can look forward to developing a pattern of interdependence – that is, a mutual reliance on each other. It's a feeling – a knowing – that there's somebody in your corner and you can say "my partner has my back."

There are so many times when I've known that Joseph had my back, including an incident when some people were telling lies about me. He knew it because what they were saying was so far from anything he'd ever known me to say or do. It was clear that the people were working to tarnish my integrity, something very important to me. I was very upset and really hurt.

After doing some research, Joseph called the two people who supposedly started the lies. Neither could say where they got their information (of course not, because they were lies). Joseph let the parties involved know, in no uncertain terms, that they had to stop spreading false rumors. After he had those tough conversations, to the best of my knowledge, the lies stopped. What Joseph did made me feel like I wasn't alone; he had my back.

Also, during the year when I was helping my mother get her house ready for sale, I knew Joseph was in my corner. First, he was with me each week helping me fix her house up. Then, when my mother got upset about the upheaval, he had a way of calming her down. He was there every step of the way; my siblings were not. If it wasn't for Joseph, I would have been taking care of my mother all on my own.

When you have the knowledge that someone has your back and they're in your corner – when you know it and see it and feel it – the result *has to be* true intimacy. *How could it not?*

AVOID AT ALL COSTS

On the other side of the behavioral coin, and in the same way that there are "must have" traits for a Five-Year Marriage, there are also "avoid at all costs" behaviors. Some of these might be fun in an affair or short term relationship. They might also kick up your adrenaline and make you feel like you're living "on the edge." That can be (sort of) exciting in the short term but not healthy for the long term. In fact, they are behaviors that can be disastrous for your Five-Year Marriage.

Four of the most common detrimental negative behaviors in a relationship, and ones that have absolutely no place in a Five-Year Marriage, are:

Addiction
Addiction means having a compulsion toward one particular activity. Someone's addiction, before you realize it's an addiction, can actually be fun. The person who likes to drink might seem like a fun partier who knows how to have a good time. It doesn't bother you that s/he drinks too much because you're enjoying going to various bars, meeting new people, and other fun things. However, it's usually only fun at the beginning when you are still infatuated. Sadly, addictive behaviors get old fast.

Addiction includes a cadre of behaviors that do not support the Five-Year Marriage. *It does not matter what the addiction is*: food, alcohol, drugs, gambling, bulimia, sex, work, or anything else. If your partner is addicted, that means that s/he has one focus – getting the next fix. The focus isn't where it should be – on you, your relationship and your shared goals and dreams. *It never will be.*

While some addictions can be easy to spot, many addicts are high-functioning. That means a person can go about daily life and conceal the addiction for a long time. Some alcoholics only drink on the weekends. Some drug addicts use their drug of choice to enhance performance. They're uber-creative or they seem to be tireless, and they are an asset to the job or relationship.

I know one woman who has a high-level position in her company. She doesn't drink on the job, but she starts drinking as soon as she gets home. It's not unusual for her to go through a bottle of wine in an evening, and to do it several times a week. Friday night is a party that ends when she calls a car service to take her home from the bar. Saturday lunch begins with a glass of wine and doesn't stop until her conversation is incomprehensible. However, when Monday morning rolls around, she's back at work, functioning well and doing her job.

High-functioning addicts aren't easy to detect. But addictions, no matter what they are, are costly. And it's not just financial. For everyone around the addict, there is untold stress, both dealing with the addict and handling the addictive behaviors.

If you aren't sure if your prospective partner has an addiction, but you suspect something's going on, start looking for missing chunks of time that don't have a good explanation. Or a money shortage that doesn't make any sense. Don't dismiss your gut feeling as a lack of trust, lack of loyalty, self-blame, or anything else that says you are making a mountain out of a molehill, even though the addict will tell you that you are.

Addicts are often good at masking the behavior and giving the appearance of being in possession of all seven "must-have" behaviors. But the act cannot continue indefinitely.

Addiction becomes a third partner in a relationship, a life-sucking partner.

In the Five-Year Marriage, there is only room for you, your partner and the life you are creating together. Addiction is out.

Do you notice addictive tendencies or have any of your family or friends noticed something and mentioned it to you?

Narcissism

Narcissism seems to be rampant these days. The quirky thing about narcissists is that they often don't appear, at first, to be self-centered. In fact, in the beginning, a narcissist can make you feel like you are really, *really* important. S/he can even tell you that you "saved" them – for example, you saved them from the pain of the last relationship, or from being lonely, and more. That's because the narcissist, in the early stages, sees you as an extension of his or her own self. It's as though his/her sun is shining on you, and the narcissistic light s/he exudes warms you and makes you feel good.

Until that brightness dims or sparkles in another direction. *And it always does.*

At some point you start to notice that, when s/he tells a story, s/he is at the center of the action and looking good. In fact, every story convinces you that s/he is the best at everything: the best participant at some sport or in some meeting, the best cook, knows the best people, gives the best advice, is the best at helping people, motivating others, solving problems, and on and on. Also, s/he has a habit of trying to top everyone else's stories with a personal best story.

In the early stages of your relationship, you pretend not to mind. You ignore any negative feelings when the red flags and screeching warning bells going off in your head. After all, the way s/he acts makes you feel good – like you're part of something bigger. You like it; it's part of the attraction.

Before too long, however, the narcissistic tendencies intensify. Conversations now focus on the latest fabulous thing s/he did – in everything from a workplace task to making hamburgers on the grill. When a conversation focuses on you or anyone else, s/he interjects a comment that shifts the focus back to him/her.

Over time s/he ignores your boundaries and doesn't keep promises. S/he acts as though the rules are for others; s/he believes s/he can get away with anything.

Gradually, the sunlight that once made you feel so good starts fading until you are left out of the equation. You wonder what you did that changed things.

Narcissism is a personality disorder defined by Merriam-Webster as "egoism" and "excessive concern for oneself with or without exaggerated feelings of self-importance." According to the Mayo Clinic, "Narcissistic Personality Disorder involves arrogant behavior, a lack of empathy for other people, and a need for admiration – all of which must be consistently evident at work and in relationships. People who are narcissistic are frequently described as cocky, self-centered, manipulative, and demanding." [22]

As your partner's sense of self-entitlement and self-importance grows around you, you begin to feel shut off. S/he becomes high maintenance. You find it exhausting.

When you stop blaming yourself for not being able to live up to the narcissist's expectations, you get weary of the counter-productive behaviors. You try to discuss your feelings but, unfortunately, a person with narcissistic tendencies is very thin-skinned. S/he doesn't take well to criticism, even when it's constructive.

In the Five-Year Marriage, narcissism means you won't problem-solve very well. Every effort to express your feelings, if those feelings don't shine a positive light on your partner, are met with anger and/or condescension. Eventually you feel muzzled.

As a result, the whole focus of your relationship is making your partner feel good. You have no voice. You feel bad – about the relationship and yourself.

Narcissism is too much work in the Five-Year Marriage, which is already hard enough. Do you want to make extra work for yourself?[23]

Domestic Abuse
Domestic abuse is always about power and control. It usually includes various forms of physical, verbal, and emotional mistreatment. Early signs of physical abuse could include pushing, shoving, and outright hitting. It might even show itself as control over money, if lack of money takes away from basic needs.

Verbal abuse comes in the form of constant criticism, vile name calling, accusations, blaming, and even demeaning jokes. Even withholding information can sometimes be considered verbal abuse. However it is delivered, verbal abuse is designed to humiliate or degrade.

Emotional abuse is a behavior which is designed to destabilize your personal power and self-esteem. It's marked by behaviors such as bullying, intimidation, shaming, and other actions that undermine a partner's confidence.

In my book, *Victorious Woman! Shaping Life's Challenges into Personal Victories*, I told Lilly's and Nancy's stories of domestic abuse. Lilly, the soft-spoken fourth child in her Puerto Rican family, was a classic good girl. Her mother suffered from a debilitating lung disease and, through most of Lilly's teenage years, she was her mother's caregiver. When her mother died, at age forty-seven, Lily felt lost. It wasn't long before she met "a slightly older man who wore nice suits, looked good and 'knew stuff.'" Lilly fell in love with him almost immediately. He quickly exerted control, moving Lilly out of town, and far away from her siblings and friends.

In the years that followed, Lilly wasn't allowed to talk to her family unless her spouse was around. While he came up with one get-rich-quick scheme after another, he made Lilly work in minimum-wage jobs; he controlled the money. If Lilly didn't follow his orders, there was hell to pay.

Nancy's story was similar. She married a divorced man with three children and moved from Virginia to Pennsylvania. Nancy said her life revolved around "running the household according to the dictates of her controlling husband. He drank heavily and, by the time she had three children of her own, she became increasingly more frightened for her safety and the safety of the children."

Looking back, both Lilly and Nancy said the seeds of domestic abuse were present while they were dating. However, both said they were too naïve to realize it.

Each of the women left their abusive relationships, but only after years of abuse. When they did, both Lilly and Nancy became single mothers without financial input from the abusers.

If abuse happens in a Five-Year Marriage, you have a better opportunity to extricate yourself from an abusive man or woman. Also, presuming you figured out child custody and divorce finances before you entered into the marriage, you might have an easier time getting through a divorce.

However, why go through that? An abusive man or woman will almost always give some hint of abusiveness, even before the engagement. Isolation is a tool the abuser employs to limit contact with friends and family. The abuser will stalk you when you aren't with him or her. S/he will distract you from your family and friends and find ways to distance them from you.

If, while dating, you aren't sure if you are in an abusive relationship, the internet provides a plethora of information. In addition, movies like *Sleeping with the Enemy, What's Love Got to Do with It,* and *The Burning Bed* each describe life with a controlling spouse who makes irrational demands on the person they profess to love. When those demands aren't met, the control freak spouse meets out a variety of punishments.

All domestic abuse does is suck the life out of your soul. It's better to pay attention before you make a commitment. Learn the signs and notice it from the beginning; quit while you're ahead.[24]

Sociopathy
The Sociopath is much like the narcissist, except that sociopathy is narcissism on steroids.

Sociopaths are pathological liars who are usually very smart, glib, and successful. Many sociopaths are charmers and exhibit overt sexual behaviors.

When you meet a sociopath, you are likely to think you've found your perfect match. S/he can convince you of everything and talk you into anything that satisfies some bizarre selfish need. To say the sociopath is manipulative is an understatement.

One of the telltale signs of sociopathy is that, when s/he gets caught in a lie, s/he is likely to brush it off like it's no big deal. To the sociopath, it isn't.

Sometimes a sociopath will fake remorse. S/he can even get away with that for a while. Eventually it becomes clear that it's an act, and there is a distinct lack remorse or guilt.

In the early 1990s there was the famous Long Island, New York, case that attracted worldwide attention and sparked a media frenzy. A teenager, Amy Fisher, was in love with the married, thirty-something Joey Buttafuoco. One day Amy drove to Joey's house and knocked on the door. When Joey's spouse, Mary Jo, opened the door, Amy shot Mary Jo in the face.

Mary Jo survived the shooting. For years, living with a bullet lodged in her head, she believed the story of innocence that her high school sweetheart and spouse of twenty-plus years insisted was true. Mary Jo and Joey were on all the news magazine shows. They were even the consultants for a made-for-TV movie about what happened to Mary Jo. All the while, Mary Jo defended Joey.

Unfortunately, Joey's story was a lie. He was indicted on nineteen counts of statutory rape, sodomy, and endangering the welfare of a child. He eventually pleaded guilty and served jail time.

In 2009, Mary Jo wrote *Getting It Through My Thick Skull: Why I Stayed, What I Learned, and What Millions of People Involved with Sociopaths Need to Know*. She wanted to tell her story, but she also wanted to inform others about the perils of living with a sociopath. Mary Jo wrote that, after the couple divorced, it was her son who told her the hard truth about her ex-husband. Mary Jo said that, at first, she couldn't believe what her son was saying. She was stunned by the peculiar revelation.

So, that night, Mary Jo spent a few hours doing internet research. That's when, she said, "the lights went on." She says she learned "the missing piece to an infuriating puzzle." It answered decades-old questions in her mind that included, "Why was our marriage in such constant turmoil?" and "Why was I continually off-balance and bewildered?"

Interestingly, most sociopaths *can* have long-term relationships and even marriages. In fact, the average sociopath probably has several of them. That's likely because, for the partner of a sociopath, it takes about five years to figure out that you're in a bad situation. It could take much longer to come to terms with your own disillusionment and then disentangle and get free. For Mary Jo, it was thirty years.

Save yourself the trouble. Sociopaths are very definitely not made for the Five-Year Marriage.[25]

Evaluating Must-Haves and Avoid-at-All-Costs
Before looking at your prospective Five-Year Marriage partner, do some self-evaluation. Are *you* the kind of person who would be a good Five-Year Marriage Partner? If you are, what makes you a good partner? If not, *how* not?

If you are a good partner, you will be focused on *be*-ing the person who has most (or all!) of the "must-haves" and none of the "avoid" behaviors. It's the smartest thing you can do for yourself if you want a Five-Year Marriage partnership. Why? Because when *you* are the best partner for a Five-Year Marriage, you are most likely to seek and attract the same kind of partner.

Next, when you are considering a Five-Year Marriage, take time to notice if your prospective partner has the seven "must-have" behaviors. Nobody, including you, has to be perfect. But your partner has to have (at least) a decent sensibility for things like personal responsibility and fairness. That's what you need to build the energy and the vision that has the strongest potential for creating a solid Five-Year Marriage.

Keep in mind that looks and passion change over time. When they do, all those "must-have" traits start to shine. Being able to have a conversation and a respectful disagreement with someone or knowing that person is there for you in a pinch – those things become very, very attractive, even sexy.

Meanwhile, the "avoid at all costs" behaviors can become killers (sometimes literally!).

In the next chapter, *Five-Year Marriage Basics: The Beginnings*, you will be delving into your own thoughts and feelings and sharing them with your prospective partner. Then you'll get to *The Nitty Gritty* chapter where you'll start sorting out the details of your Five-Year Marriage agreement.

Best wishes as you continue this adventure!

Chapter Three: Joseph's Take

When Annmarie and I got married the first time, I'm not sure I understood the partnership part of marriage. I had a very small comfort zone then. I don't think I even got it during our second Five-Year Marriage. It wasn't until we started talking about our shared values that things really started to work.

Since then, having Annmarie as a partner has helped me to, step by step, increase my confidence and get out of my tiny comfort zone box. I doubt I'd have a successful massage therapy practice if Annmarie and I weren't in our marriage as partners. Some things I couldn't have done alone.

It's the same with Annmarie. I know Annmarie agrees that there are things she's done that couldn't have happened without us being partners.

I like that Annmarie and I are team. Becoming a team wasn't easy and it took time. But it's made a difference to me and to our relationship.

Chapter Four
Five-Year Marriage Basics:
The Beginnings

The goal in marriage is not to think alike,
but to think together.
Robert C. Dodds, Psychologist and Marriage Counselor

Movies, like life, are a long time in the making. In a film, actors bring a bunch of words written on paper to life. Sometimes the film doesn't quite work, and a script doctor is called in. The script doctor helps make parts of the story stronger or make the lines fit the purpose of the story's intent more effectively. The edits enhance the characters' lines but it's still up to the actors to deliver the lines so that they are believable. If the actors can't do that, the movie might go straight to DVD.

The Five-Year Marriage contract does for your marriage what a script doctor does for a film. It helps you edit out the parts that are weak, the things that aren't working. It enhances what is good and enables each of you to be your best.

However, like a film, you begin with something on paper. It's basic.

After the lust of being lovers dies down (and it will), you want to know you two have the promising propensity to be best friends. That's what you'll be doing in this chapter. It's designed to help you figure out if you and your prospective partner are the right cast mates for your Five-Year Marriage. It will help ensure that you aren't giving your relationship some "spin" or "hype" just to feel good. That's why it's *The Beginnings* of the Five-Year Marriage Basics.

When I first suggested the idea of a Five-Year Marriage, neither Joseph nor I had any idea what it would mean or how challenging it would be. We didn't get into figuring out five-year contracts at the beginning. The most negotiating and contracting we did was whatever was involved in the process of buying our first house.

What I knew then was that Joseph and I travelled well together, both literally and figuratively. It wasn't the same as hanging out with my girlfriends. His testosterone energy was unlike the estrogen energy of my friends. I liked the blend of our energies. It felt satisfying.

However, by that time I was old enough and had seen enough to know that being friends in a marriage is important. I had enough experience in life and our relationship to appreciate Joseph's dependability. I could feel we had at least the seeds of the other "must-haves" and felt safe that the "avoids" weren't part of our relationship.

Still, I needed more.

Throughout my adult life, I've been a big believer in having a vision and goals backed up by a plan. So I told Joseph that's what I wanted to do with him too. It seemed to make sense.

Joseph was readily on board with both. Before we had our first wedding, we took time to figure out what we wanted together.

With just that (our vision, a couple rudimentary goals, and our plan), during our first Five-Year Marriage, we got through the typical newlywed challenges of money, privacy/space, handling responsibilities, and the other challenges that most couples experience.

After five years, and because we still liked each other and got along well, we decided to marry again. What Joseph and I didn't understand then was the value of revisiting our previous vision and goals and revising our plan. When we decided to marry again we were still using the same vision and plan we created at the beginning, even though quite a few things had changed.

That second marriage might have been our last one if it wasn't for our five-year commitment. When, in our second marriage, we hit that aforementioned "wall," Joseph and I got stuck. We tried fixing it by talking about it, arguing about it, and applying problem-solving techniques I read about in books. Nothing worked. In fact, things got worse.

I remember clearly and painfully my breakthrough night. Joseph and I had yet another screaming match that ended with us in separate rooms. In my case, it was the living room. In the early morning hours that followed a sleepless night in the recliner, it came to me. We either had to get help or, at the end of that marriage, we would have to break up.

When I told Joseph we had to get help, he wasn't very happy at the idea of going outside our relationship for help. Yet the time-sensitivity of our Five-Year Marriage pushed us forward.

Seeing a marriage counselor wasn't easy on our egos or emotions. Both of us believed we were justified in our feelings. Both of us were "right." Neither of us wanted to admit that we needed to do something else.

Seeing a counselor wasn't easy on our finances either. With both of us in the early years of our own businesses, and having experienced a couple of financial setbacks, money was tight.

Still, though we hated the idea of going "outside" for help, we had enough love to want to work it out. We also had enough willingness to find and fix the problem. So, though it meant giving up some other things, we were willing to spend the money.

When we went to that first appointment with Ralph, the marriage counselor who was recommended by a friend, it was with intention. We both knew that if we couldn't fix the problem, we weren't going to keep going. We didn't want to break up, but we would have, without help. That "wall" was something we couldn't seem to get around, over, or through, and it was too ugly to keep up. We either had to tear it down or walk away.

During the months we were in therapy, we dug deep into ourselves as well as our relationship. Leaning on Ralph's guidance, Joseph and I had hours of conversations either on long walks in our neighborhood or at a local Barnes and Noble. What we did then became the process that now precedes each of our marriages. It was a demanding and uncomfortable place for both of us, both individually and as a couple. What we learned was eye-opening and interesting.

Those early practices got easier over time. They aren't quite as challenging now as during those difficult days in our second marriage. Now we're used to the discomfort of a difficult conversation, the disagreement that comes with hammering something out, and the amount of time it sometimes takes to get to agreement.

Though we're used to the process, I can't honestly say it's easy. Still, we know what happens on the other side. We also know it's worth the effort.

What got started during our second marriage is what I'm sharing with you. *The Beginnings* described here, along with the information in the next couple of chapters, give you a process, a method, for choosing and contracting with your Five-Year Marriage partner. Putting these essential ideas into practice will help you figure out what you what both want in your Five-Year Marriage.

Admittedly, this step won't be easy; it's not meant to be. Yet it's one of the most valuable things you'll do for yourself and each other.

In the pages that follow you'll be going deep into your own thoughts and feelings. Then, when you've figured out what's going on inside you, next you'll be revealing those thoughts and feelings to someone else.

Following this process can be emotionally risky – and that will be true whether you've known each other for six months or thirty years. But marriage – any marriage – is risky. And that's especially true with your Five-Year Marriage.

Three things to remember as you sort out your thoughts and share them with your partner:

- *Right* does not mean perfect. *Right* means right *for you*. In my experiences, I've noticed that most people aren't very clear about what "right" is for them.
- It's not about the partner but about the relationship. You aren't looking to critique each other's thoughts or ideas. Everyone is entitled to their own thoughts and feelings. What you are

looking for is the synergy – that emotional chemistry – that makes a good relationship.

- You are working toward a good foundation for putting together your Five-Year Marriage contract.

Here's why it's important: you probably say – to yourself and others – something like, "I want a happy marriage." Unfortunately, "happy marriage" is just not enough, and for a very simplistic reason. If you say you want a happy marriage, do you know what a "happy marriage" means to you? Does s/he?

Can you describe it? Can s/he?

Chances are you can't. Try it. Take out a piece of paper and write down fifteen things that make a happy marriage. How long does it take you to think of fifteen characteristics of a happy marriage?

Now, keep in mind, a marriage is two people. When you think of a "happy marriage," how do you know if that nebulous model noodling around in your head – or any of those fifteen things you wrote down – is the same as the marriage model your partner has?

Unless you have long conversations about what marriage is, you won't know. When the average couple agree that they both want a "happy marriage," there's a better than 50% chance that they're talking about two entirely dissimilar experiences. *She* might be thinking about snuggling together on a Friday night or having a house full of babies. Meanwhile, *he's* thinking about having regular sex and being loved and respected without doing anything to get those. Or, maybe he's the one thinking about the babies and snuggling, and *she's* focused on her career and thinking he can be a stay-at-home dad.

If you and your partner can't articulate your expectations, how do you know your prospective partner doesn't have a completely dissimilar outlook? *You don't.*

It's like saying you want to go out for a good dinner for your birthday. You're thinking about a thick, juicy steak but your partner takes you out for burgers. You're disappointed and, knowing you are, your partner is upset. You thought you were getting what you wanted and s/he thought s/he was giving you a special treat. At the end of the night, neither of you is feeling the love.

Complicating the whole progression are the much-celebrated celebrity flings and the ever-satisfying and always optimistic romance novels. Without realizing it, you and your partner are programmed to think about love and marriage in terms of glamour and pizzazz. Many couples enter dating relationships in a Fifty Shades-style "lover takes all" fantasy that demands that one person give away his or her personal power to the other.

Unfortunately, those expectations are designed to support only a short-term tryst, like the kind you see in a one-hour television drama or a ninety-minute movie. Those aren't happy marriages; they're illusions. That's why so many celebrity relationships fizzle out long before the five-year mark.

Whenever one partner gives away his/her personal power to the other, all the responsibility for creating happiness is on one person. Over time it becomes dissatisfying for both partners. What happens is that one partner feels trapped. Meanwhile, it's too much pressure for the "power partner" to keep it up. Eventually the "magic" dissipates. What's left is a harsh reality with an unhappy ending.

That's why the Five-Year Marriage is so individually distinctive.

For the Five-Year Marriage, BE-ing the right person means knowing yourself and knowing what you need and want to make yourself happy and satisfied. No matter what happens in life, no matter who comes and who goes, the only constant relationship you have now, have had, and will have in the future is the one you have with yourself. If you can't know, like, and be happy with yourself now, how can you know, like, and be happy with someone else – for five years or for any period of time?

If like attracts like, *and it does*, BE-ing the right person will take you closer to being with your "right" person. When you are, you and your partner can discover where you both are, mentally and emotionally, at this time of your life, and what you're good at – and not-so-good at.

By working through the sections that follow, you'll get greater clarity around what you need and want in your marriage. That's very basic but really valuable information.

Just in case you're thinking about bypassing *The Beginnings* chapter, consider this: you're buying a new television. You start looking and find hundreds of options to choose from – big screens, smart TVs, networked…it's an electronics maze. If you go online or into the store without knowing what you need and want and what options are important to you, you're likely to get something that isn't a good fit for you. Then, for the five years you own that television, every time you want to do something with it, you feel disappointed, ticked off and stuck.

You don't want the same thing to happen in your Five-Year Marriage.

To make it easier for you, I separated your marriage "discovery" into two sections: Buzzwords (Part I) and Headlights (Part II).

As you look at the questions for these sections, you might think, "Wow, this takes a lot of time," or "These questions are making me feel uncomfortable," and "I don't want to go through all this; I just want to get married."

Before you think about bowing out of this process, here are some things to consider:

- Yes, it will take a lot of time now. However, it will take considerably less time, and be less stressful now than if you wait and have to sort out the same kinds of issues in a divorce.
- Yes, some of the questions could make you feel uncomfortable. That's common. So what? Isn't it better that you're uncomfortable now instead of later when the stakes are higher and it's more complicated?

- If you don't want to go through all this, then maybe the Five-Year Marriage isn't for you. You're better off going the traditional route.

Here's something else to consider: as you boldly, persistently, and *lovingly* work through this process, you'll give yourself and your partner a starting point and a point of reference.

When you're finished the inside thinking work and the outside sharing, you'll have a clearer "big picture" of what your life will be like as loving Five-Year Marriage partners. From it you'll be shaping not only your partnership, but the next five years of your life. Also, you'll be able to use it to notice your progress and score your wins.

Of course, your conversations may also show you that you would make terrible Five-Year Marriage partners. That would be hard to deal with now. At the same time, it could save you both years of heartache and heartbreak.

So what you do in this chapter will form the foundation and give you the proper footing for exploring the next chapter, the *"Five-Year Marriage Basics: The Nitty Gritty"* of specific contract details.

So get started…and best wishes for many rewarding heart-to-hearts!

PART I – Buzzwords

You'll do this part by yourself. Answering the questions will help you figure out things like your personal idea for your Five-Year Marriage's purpose, vision, and goals. As you work through the sections, you'll probably find yourself coming up with common words or themes. Those buzzwords will eventually help you shortcut many future conversations.

This section includes four segments:
- Why Be Married? (purpose)
- Think Ahead (vision and goals)
- Communication Styles (friendship)
- Complementary Skills (partnership)

Make sure you give Part I plenty of on-your-own time for stress-free daydreaming, visualizing, and expressing. If you try to do it fast, chances are you'll be answering from your brain instead of your heart.

As you work through these questions, first by yourself, and the again with your partner, create a reasonable timeline and deadlines for yourselves. For example, set aside two weeks to work on the questions alone. Write the answers down and look them over. As you take notes, it's a good idea to keep all your observations in some kind of journal or copybook (versus in some file on your computer). Yes, you *can* keep everything on your tablet or phone, but sometimes this kind of noodling is helped by doodling.

Next, set up some dates for the two of you to talk about each segment. *I suggest five dates, one for each part.* When you only have to talk about one topic at a time, it'll be easier to have those conversations. Also, "buzzwords" will start becoming noticeable and you'll have plenty of time to explore the "headlight" ideas that come up.

Let's get going!

Purpose: Why Be Married?

1. Why do I want to be married? Everybody has reasons for choosing marriage. You could just live together, but you're planning a marriage. Why? Here are some possibilities:
   - I'm tired of being alone.
   - I've been having a great time being single but now I want more.
   - I want to have children (or I have children) and I want to raise them in a two-parent home.
   - I want to prove to myself/others that I'm [fill in the blank: mature-stable-responsible-etc.].
   - Marriage will get my parents off my back.
   - All my friends are married and I feel left out.
   - All my friends are living together and I don't see that as the best lifestyle for me.

2. What matters most to me in a relationship? List your relationship values in order, starting with the one that is most important. Some examples could be: physical intimacy, emotional intimacy, trust, commitment, honesty, safety, fidelity, love, affection, good hygiene, patience. See FiveYearMarriage.com for Annmarie Kelly's Values List

3. Is there a difference between how I view a relationship compared to a marriage? For example, do I see dating someone as a fun but relatively short-lived experience and a marriage as a lifestyle or a job? Or are relationships more easy-going, while marriage is an obligation?

4. What does a happy and successful relationship look like to me? Based on my past relationships, what made them good or bad for me? What would I want more of, and what would I want less of - or not at all - in my current or future relationships?

5. In the past, when a relationship started to go sour, what was the first thing I noticed?

6. Thinking of marriages I admire and ones I don't, what does a happy and successful marriage look like to me? Why? That is, what was good about them that I want to duplicate and what wasn't that I don't want to repeat?

7. How do I want to be treated during my Five-Year Marriage?

8. Considering all the family I have (my family, his/her family, children, and the family we have together), how important is family to me? Why?

9. I know why I want to be married, but why do I want to marry [partner's name]?

Vision and Goals: Thinking into My Future

1. What is the intention for this marriage, that is, why are we together?
   - That we love each other goes without saying. But what else do I want us to have together? Do I see us as "better together" and more powerful, stable, stronger, and/or solid than what I or we have now?

2. How do I see my life playing out over the next five years?
   - When, five years from now, I'm looking back on this marriage, what do I hope I'm saying about what we did together? Would I want to say our relationship was about: safe sex, romance, companionship, children, family, travelling partner, better finances, status, or something else?

   It's really important to know what you want. If you don't have a clear picture of what you want going *into* the Five-Year Marriage, you will definitely not get it *during* your Five-Year Marriage. And, as a result, are less likely to continue into another Five-Year Marriage with the same partner.

3. What can I *reasonably* expect from my partner?
   - Are you expecting affection, fidelity, sharing the finances, safety, children, financial growth, spiritual growth, a health-focused lifestyle, fairness…whatever you expect, write it down.
   - Then, pick your top ten expectations.
   - Share your expectations with your partner. Which ones come up on both of your "top ten" lists? Do you have similar lists, or are your expectations opposite?

4. How do I see us…
   - Sharing the household responsibilities? Will we have equal but different responsibilities inside and outside? Will one of us be a stay-at-home parent while the other

works outside the home – maybe not at first, but after we have children?

- Dividing the financial responsibilities? Will we blend our accounts and pay all the bills together? Or will we keep our own accounts and just split the bill-paying? If we go separately, how often will we share financial information, including looking at each other's annual credit reports?

- Separating out the family and friend responsibilities, including our in-laws and our children? For example, how will we keep up with our friends? Will be both be OK if each of us has a girls' or guys' night out? Am I more comfortable with couples' dates, or having everyone to our house for potluck dinners, or something different?

- How do I see us making social arrangements with our friends and our families? Will one of us be the go-to person for organizing holidays or birthdays, including sending cards?

Connection: Exploring Your Communication Styles

1. How would I describe my communication style *most* of the time?
   - Showing and conducting
   - Interacting and sharing
   - Steady and stable
   - Cautious and detailed

2. Am I the kind of person who wants to talk things out or do I just want to move on to something else?

3. When I need to discuss something, am I the kind of person who wants to get everything out on the table right away, or do I need

time to process before discussing? Or do I not want to discuss anything and just let things work themselves out?

4. When I'm upset with the topic, am I more likely to push the discussion to get more clarity, or, because I don't want to talk about it, am I more likely to stonewall?

5. Can we argue effectively? Are there too many times when an argument escalates into raised voices and ends in a stalemate? Does one of us end the argument by walking away with no resolution? Do we get distracted by bringing up old stuff and pointing fingers, and then we don't get to the problem that started the argument?

6. During an argument, what would be more important to me: being right, keeping the peace, or finding a shared solution?

7. What have I noticed is our biggest communication challenge so far?

8. How do I deal with change? How does it seem that s/he deals with change?

Partnership: Finding Complementary Skills

1. What skills and talents do I bring to the relationship? I'm good at:
    - Organizing (the house, social engagements, etc.)
    - Doing the finances (figuring out a budget, paying the bills, investing)
    - Being persistent
    - Always following through on a project and not allowing myself to get distracted or sidetracked
    - Researching (products, ideas, etc.)
    - Nurturing and being supportive
    - Being creative and thinking outside the box
    - Other strengths: sharing, staying focused, creativity, risk-taking, following directions, willingness to learn,

creativity, strong work ethic, supportive…the list can go on and on…

2. How do my skills contribute to solving problems?
   - If I say my skillset is one that's good for problem-solving, does that mean I'm the one who is better at that, *or do I just think I am?* What does my partner think?
   - If I'm the better problem solver, am I open to listening to other options, even when I know my partner isn't as good at problem solving as I am?
   - If I'm not the better problem solver, am I willing to accept my partner's solution?

3. How do my talents merge with my partner's talents?
   - If I'm really good at budgets and bills, and my partner is good at research, one of us can organize the family finances while the other figures out things like which is the best cable plan or most efficient appliance.
   - If one of us is creative and the other is better at staying focused, one of us can keep us on track toward a goal while the other is solving problems as they come up.

To be realistic and fair, some of the ways your skills complement each other probably won't show up until you've lived together for a while. Still, getting a sense of how some of your skills complement each other now will help you sort out your agreements later.

In addition, your skills will develop and grow. Sorting skills and talents out now doesn't mean you can't learn or get better at some skill. You will grow and mature and change. You might not be assertive at this point, but time and effort will change that. You will want that change to be reflected in your Five-Year Marriage.

Joan was a smart and clever but slightly sheltered young woman when, at twenty-one, she married a man who was almost ten years older. He was already in business, socially connected, and always seemed to know what to do. He ran the show and, early on, that was fine with Joan.

By the time Joan turned twenty-six, she had learned a thing or two. She no longer felt comfortable with her spouse always being in charge. She wanted more of a say in what the couple did. However, their patterns were set and there was no changing them. The couple divorced but continued to be friends until his death a few years ago.

During a 2016 conversation with Joan, she reflected on that marriage with an interesting insight. "If there was a Five-Year Marriage then," Joan thoughtfully revealed, "I don't think we would have gotten a divorce." With a Five-Year Marriage, Joan believes that they could have restructured their decision-making and problem-solving to reflect her growing maturity. And they would have stayed married.

Part II - Headlights

A headlight is a beam of light that leads the way forward. Sharing your thoughts with your partner will be that beam of light for your Five-Year Marriage planning. So once you answer the "buzzwords" questions by yourself, share your answers and thoughts with your partner. This "headlight" conversation will help you both move through unrealistic expectations and shared shortcomings. Understand that you aren't likely to agree on everything. However, you are likely to have some very interesting conversations.

NOTE: It's better to have "headlight" conversations – and arguments – now. If you disagree now you have time to learn how to work out your differences. As you do, you'll be better able to get on the same page going forward. Or not go forward.

For some reason, as mentioned earlier, most people don't think of marriage as a partnership. But it is and it includes a contract, even though, most of the time, the contract is unspoken. What is dangerous about having that sort of contract is that the "unspoken" part is not mutually agreed upon by both parties. Consequently, it creates a presumption that is often the source of plenty of hurt and anger between couples.

That's why, once you have both gone through all four sections alone, you share your answers with your partner. How well you share your words and your heart isn't just important. It can be telling, emotional, and even cathartic. This sharing starts the formation of your Five-Year Marriage contract. And, when you make that emotional connection, it can be better than holding hands or having romance.

A chance encounter reminded me of the importance of the "sharing" part of this process.

When I was writing the *Five-Year Marriage*, I was often distracted by my regular work with the Victorious Woman Project. I wasn't getting enough uninterrupted time to write. So I decided to sequester myself in a hotel in Gettysburg, Pennsylvania, in late December. Unlike most other months, due to the cold, Gettysburg isn't much of a tourist destination at that time of year.

One morning, I was alone at a table in the hotel's very crowded breakfast room. There was a shortage of tables and I was sitting alone when Sylvia asked if she could join me. I nodded and pointed to the seat across from me; I was happy for the company.

Over Belgian waffles, yogurt, and tea, I found out that Sylvia and her spouse were celebrating their fiftieth anniversary by travelling from New York to Florida. The road trip was a driving adventure that included all the places they'd wanted to visit, but until then, hadn't. Gettysburg was one of those places.

As we chatted, I told Sylvia I was traveling alone so I could write the Five-Year Marriage undisturbed. She was intrigued by the five-year idea. We talked about marriage and its complexities. We both agreed that marriage is the hardest thing either one of us have ever done.

Then I asked the retired business owner and mother of two for her secret to being married for fifty years. She didn't miss a beat when she told me communication was big – *very big.*

Sylvia revealed that communication wasn't easy in the early years of her marriage. She explained that she and her spouse were both very young (nineteen and twenty-one) on their wedding day. Simply being so young created its own challenges for the newlyweds.

In those early days, and while raising their two sons, Sylvia said she and her spouse "didn't always see eye to eye." She said it took her "some years" before she learned to speak up and express what she wanted...*and be willing fight for it if she had to do so.* For a woman married in the 1960s, when feminism was in its infancy and Gloria Steinem was just getting her activist life on track, women were mostly still expected to be "seen but not heard" wives.

Once feminism took hold, most women didn't have an easy time of making their opinions heard. It wasn't uncommon for a woman to have to "learn" how to express her feelings or "fight" for what she wanted.

What took Sylvia and her spouse many years to be able to do is what you're doing now. You'll have the opportunity – and the obligation – to express your needs and desires. You'll be thinking about what you want and then talking about it with your partner. And you'll be able to do it before you are in a relationship where you have to "fight for it."

The goal you're after here is the formation of a **shared vision, your Five-Year Marriage goals** and a **mutually agreed upon plan** for the next five years. The only way you can respectfully do that is by talking about what you both want and expect. And, between two people, it's something that doesn't happen by magic. It takes time and effort.

However, those conversations will frame the choices and resulting decisions that will become the heart and soul of your contract. All the details are important, but they will mean nothing if they don't hang on your **shared vision, your Five-Year Marriage goals**, and a **mutually agreed upon plan**.

Admittedly, talking about visions and the resulting goals and plans isn't as much fun as talking about the songs you want your DJ to play at your wedding or where you'll go for a honeymoon. Just keep in mind that all the planning for a wedding is over in one day. All the planning for your Five-Year Marriage will last you for (at least) five years.

Ready?

Here are the basic Ground Rules for Beginners:

- **Time:** Make an appointment to have a Family Meeting. It could be every Sunday at noon or every other Monday night from 7-8:30pm. There's something about having a definite time and a specific topic that gives the process an air of importance. Also, knowing the topic and knowing you have a preparation deadline will get both of you focused.

- **Place:** Go someplace where you won't be disturbed. Book stores and cafés are good places to do this, for two reasons:
  - o It's a different environment, out of your usual setting and void of household distractions. I find that when the discussion is at home, there are enough distractions that the matters at hand don't get the full attention they need.
  - o You are less likely to argue out loud (that is, scream at each other) and more likely to keep the conversation focused on the discussion and actual problem solving.

- **Have an agenda:** Decide in advance what you are going to discuss during that meeting. It can be one topic, like how you'll handle some specific problem, or multiple topics like splitting up a household renovation and figuring how to handle the upcoming holidays. An agenda will do two things for you. It will:
  - o Help you think about what you want and what you want to say.
  - o Keep you from going in six different directions at once and ending up with nothing accomplished.

Once you know when, where and what your Family Meeting will be about, here's what to do next:

- Work with just one section from Part I at each rendezvous. Share how you responded to each of the questions in that section, one by one. It's good for you to know why your partner wants to get married and how s/he sees your future together. And understanding how your skills are shared or complementary and how you like to communicate can save you many arguments down the road.

- o Take as much time as you need to understand where your partner is coming from, what s/he is thinking. Ask questions and agree to *NOT* be defensive when your partner asks you to explain what you mean.

- o Expect that you won't agree on everything. If you're honest with each other, the conversations are likely to be emotional and can even be uncomfortable. They won't be unlike other conversations you'll have during your Five-Year Marriage. However, what you do during this sharing time can provide insight into how you handle conflict together. It will also become a foundation for future conversations. Once you are both used to the process of talking things out and get comfortable with disagreement and problem-solving, you'll be better partners together.

- o Sometimes this won't be easy, but when the small puzzle pieces don't seem to make sense, focus on the bigger picture: You're learning how to share, solve problems, and come to agreements. Your sharing conversations are providing the groundwork for your Five-Year Marriage future.

- **Slow Down:** Don't try to squeeze your sharing conversations (and, later, your contracting exchanges) into a single meeting or a single day. Think of sharing and contracting like a big rich chocolate cake. If you try to eat it all at one sitting, you're likely to make yourself sick. Maybe you won't want to have chocolate cake ever again. However, if you cut it up into pieces and savor it over several sittings, you'll get the most enjoyment from it.

- **Have a conversation.** That means two-way talk. Don't suck up all the air by not giving your partner time and space to express his/her views and thoughts.

- **You aren't alone.** Don't be afraid to ask for help from someone who knows how to help couples, like a marriage mediator or marriage counselor. Avoid asking anyone who is close to you, including parents, relatives, co-workers, or friends.

- **If you decide to get help:** Marriage Counselors and Mediators are great for helping you sort out your feelings and shine a light on things you don't even know you're saying, doing, or feeling. HOWEVER, when it comes to matters that focus on money, property, or alimony (e.g. when you are sorting out how you will care for your children should you divorce), you are better off seeking the advice of an attorney.

- Turn off your cellphone and any other devices.

Wrap-up

Once you discuss the topics, experience discomfort and have an argument (or two), hopefully you'll come to an agreement with a decent idea for where you're going together. You and your partner will also have a rhythm going between you. Both of those will help make the actual contracting part a little easier. NOTE: I say "a little" because the next step is when you roll this part into a contract or agreement that you both commit to for the next five years.

When you've finished the four segments and you believe the two of you are going in the same direction, put your decisions in a form you can use. You should be able to answer these questions:

- Why are we getting married – our purpose together?
- How do we both see the next five years playing out (joint vision)?
- What can we reasonably expect from this marriage?
- What do we want to accomplish during the next five years – individually and as partners (our personal and couple goals)?
- How will we get there (plans)?
- What are our greatest challenges – individually and as partners?
- What are our greatest strengths – individually and as partners?
- What were our personal buzzwords?

- What headlights emerged?

GOOD JOB! Now you're ready to move on to *The Nitty Gritty*! Chapter Five is waiting for you...*go for it*!

Chapter Four: Joseph's Take

I've seen many married couples grow apart because one of them has accomplished what s/he wanted but the one stayed stagnant. I didn't recognize that at the beginning of our Five-Year marriage. But now that I understand how life can get in the way, I believe that, if a couple doesn't grow together, they will grow apart.

Living the Five-Year Marriage decreases the chances of growing apart. When a couple sits down and discusses what each one wants to accomplish, what they want to learn, what hobbies they want to pursue, and more, they go in that direction together. I believe that's a necessary thing to do in order to make each one feel loved, important, and respected.

To me, this is the essence and most important reason for living a Five-Year Marriage.

Chapter Five
Five-Year Marriage Basics: The Nitty Gritty

Are you feeling a bit shaken, maybe stirred,
maybe fearful and doubtful and completely utterly, wildly terrified?
Good. Keep going.
Victoria Erickson, Author

Talk about contracts – any contract – employment, cell phone, cable, home improvement. You have a contract for everything. You make agreements when you buy a house, life insurance, and a gym membership. Sometimes even sex can have a contract.

The Big Bang Theory's Sheldon won't live with anyone who doesn't agree to a very detailed roommate contract. Not only did he demand a Roommate Agreement before living with Leonard, but when he and Amy become boyfriend and girlfriend, he created the Relationship Agreement.

In the novel, *Fifty Shades of Grey*, Christian Grey presented Anastasia Steele with a detailed dominant-submissive contract. He told her the sexual contract had to be agreed upon and signed before the couple could enter into their sadomasochistic relationship. Ana and Christian discussed each section of the sexual contract and negotiated the details of their sexual exploits.

Even after the contracting discussions, Ana thought, for a long time, about whether she wanted to enter into that kind of arrangement with Christian. Her hesitance had as much to do with the oddity of having an agreement about sex as it did about the type of sex.

Whatever you thought about the books or the movies, *Fifty Shades* opened up the idea of contracts for more than just loans and devices. Contracts for everything have become such a way of life that most people don't think twice about signing a phone contract or a contract to rent a car. You live in a contracting society.

Contracting is so run-of-the-mill that most companies you contract with have a pre-printed form ready for your signature. Even Christian Grey had a formal contract ready for Ana.

To Ana's credit, she did something most people don't do: she read and questioned everything. Most people don't (even though nearly everyone knows you should). Sometimes you find out the hard way that you didn't pay attention to the fine print; it's usually a painful lesson.

It's the same when you download a new app. How many times have you seen the message that says something like "by clicking 'continue,' you are agreeing to the terms and conditions below"? How often do you read those "terms and conditions" to which you're agreeing? Probably never. You want the app, so you click...*right*?

You aren't alone.

Here's the rub: That agreement, say with a social media site like Facebook or YouTube, tells you that your privacy isn't secure (your information goes to third parties) and, if you don't toe the line, you can lose your privileges on that site. If you don't know that, I'm betting you didn't bother to read one word of the agreement.

You've probably heard of people who have gotten kicked off a site for violating an agreement, except they often didn't know what terms they were agreeing to until there was a problem. Not knowing the terms of your agreement is a mistake.

Marriage is much the same way except the stakes are much higher.

Sometime before your wedding, you must get a marriage license. You go to City Hall and fill out some paperwork. On your wedding day, you sign the license. By doing that you enter into an agreement that signifies a lifetime of *something*. Signing your marriage license is almost like clicking the "accept" button. You don't know what *something* is, but you do it (because you want to be that person).

At the wedding, the minister or celebrant tells you the agreement is for better or for worse and you're in the marriage until you're dead. You don't know then that "till death" sometimes comes in a form other than physical. Dead sometimes happens in your heart, your spirit, or your soul.

You don't care because you're in love. You're filled with hope that you'll live the proverbial "happily ever after."

Unlike those "terms and conditions" (that you didn't read) for the app you wanted, your marriage contract spells out nothing and almost everything is left to chance. Okay, maybe you two talked about where you want to live. And how many children you want. Or maybe you talked specifically about in whose religious or spiritual practice the children will be raised. But the actual responsibilities are implied.

So how's that working out for most couples?

It is different for you.

For you and your Five-Year Marriage partner, before you "sign on the dotted line," you'll know what you are agreeing to do. You'll also know you aren't going to be married until you're dead – physically, mentally, emotionally, or spiritually. With the Five-Year Marriage, you know the end date is five years.

Still, the Five-Year Marriage isn't a guarantee. It's not perfect and you aren't perfect. But knowing what you're doing and having a mutually agreed upon vision and a plan is way better than marrying blindly.

Of course, you and your partner both have to live up to your mutual agreements. That should go without saying. *But at least you know what your agreements are!*

So, in the previous chapter, you laid the foundation for your contract. You discussed your reasons for choosing to marry and choosing each other. You acknowledged your strengths and challenges together. You shared how you see your marriage developing over the next five years.

Along the way, you also got to see how each of you handles doing the hard work of difficult communications and difficult decisions. It wasn't easy but the two of you were able to get on the same page about your marriage partnership.

That feels good, doesn't it? It gives you some feeling of safety and stability, right?

Now you can get into *The Nitty Gritty*. The clearer you and your partner get about what's what between you, and the tighter the gap is, the firmer your marriage footing will be for the next five years.

Before you start the actual work of developing your contract, discuss with each other what you expect your contract to do. In its simplest form, a contract is an agreement between two or more parties. It spells out what each contracting partner commits to and can expect from the other contracting partner(s). Little to nothing is implied, including how disputes will be resolved.

As you progress through the various areas described in this chapter, understand that you're going for *commitment with flexibility*. The commitment holds for your whole Five-Year Marriage. The flexibility enables you to rethink your agreement and adjust your contract in five years.

Commitment with flexibility acknowledges that your needs are likely to change over time. The contract or agreement you enter into today might not be a good fit five years from now. You and your life will change with each passing year. Maybe one of you gets a new job or loses a job. One of you gets an advanced degree, changes careers, becomes a stay-at-home mom or dad, coaches little league, starts a business, has a health challenge, has a parent with a health challenge.

Those are just a few of the life changes that can impact your relationship. A million things happen over the course of a lifetime. Each one of those things changes you and changes the relationship you have with others, especially the one you have with your spouse.

What makes the Five-Year Marriage distinct and very special is that those things are dealt with in five-year chunks of time.

That's what you're doing in this *"Nitty Gritty"* chapter. You're figuring out the essentials, the nuts and bolts of your life together for the next five years. Through each section, you're considering how you think and feel about this and that area of your partnership. You consider the way the various parts impact you and your life within the relationship.

While all of the contracting process can sound as though you have a strict business deal, don't let that happen. Choose instead to see contracting as an opportunity and part of the bigger picture for your Five-Year Marriage.

Here's another way to think of it…

Through your relationship, and your decision to make a life together, you and your partner have been given a beautiful and seemingly magical box. When the two of you open it, you find the box is filled with an assortment of amazing gemstones. They include gems like career, a house, children, travel, investing, or starting a business – and those are just a few you find. There are so many gems that you don't know what to do with all of them. Do you need or want them all?

You have to figure that out.

So you pick up each gemstone, one at a time, and examine it. As you hold it up to the light, you decide if there's something attractive about that gem, if it gives you something you need or want. As you look at each one, some gems will shine and you'll want them; others will have no significance.

When you're finished looking at all the baubles, you set aside the ones that are important to you *now*. The gems that you keep are the parts of your life that are important for the next five years. Maybe the ones you want now are the gems of career, housing, family, health, lifestyle, and entertainment.

Some areas aren't appropriate to your life now, e.g. parenthood or caregiving. Maybe you aren't going to have children during your first Five-Year Marriage – or ever. Also, you are years away from thinking about your parents needing care. Those are gems for another time of your life.

Or, you aren't ready or interested in making investments, traveling, or starting a small business. Those "gems" go back in the box for later. You know they're there for you if you want them, but not now. Maybe you'll want them later, in five years.

Next you look at the gems you've chosen. Lay them out on the table so you can see them all at the same time (in lieu of actual gemstones, you can write those areas on colorful index cards).

How do you want to use them during this Five-Year Marriage? How can you put them together?

One by one, you and your partner decide. Together you put them into a beautiful Five-Year Marriage setting that you both like.

What does that setting look like for you? Does it show both of you building your careers, getting promotions to senior management, buying a two-story house in a suburban development, making some long-term investments, and traveling? Or maybe that setting includes building your family structure with a couple of children in an urban location. You both see yourselves and your children enjoying the benefits of city life, including easy access to your jobs as well as an abundance of entertainment, cultural events, parks, history, museums, etc.

Using this analogy will help you see the contracting process in a "big picture/little picture" framework. Once that's done, give yourself time to let your work settle into your mind and heart. As you look at the magical arrangement of life gems, and talk about it, you'll be better able to decide if it's exactly right or if you need to rearrange the "gems." You want to be able to look at what you've done every day and feel good about it. You can see yourself and your partner actually creating that setting. If you do, *that's* how you know it's a good fit for both of you.

When it's what you want, begin to make agreements. For example, what agreements do you need to make about money and budgets to buy a house? If you aren't going to have children, what agreements do you need to make about birth control? If you are both going to pursue your careers, what agreements can you make about finding time to keep the fire burning between you instead of getting distracted with your careers? If you both want to pursue a career and have children, what agreements can you make about childcare and household duties?

Keep in mind that contracting between two people doesn't happen like magic. It takes time and effort. And it takes the kind of love that makes you willing to put it all out there for each of you to see, examine, and discuss. You *don't* want to be forced into a contract. What you *do* want is to care about and love each other enough that you want the best for yourselves individually and as a couple.

As you progress, say, in year four of this marriage, you might decide to move away from the career focus of this marriage and choose for the next Five-Year Marriage to be about children. Or you've changed jobs or careers, or you decide to start your own business. That's when some of those previously put away other gems from that "magical box" – the ones you put aside – become important. Go back and take those unused gems out and look at them again. You adjust what you've already done or create something new.

In Chapter Four, *Five-Year Marriage Basics: The Beginnings*, you developed a rhythm around having conversation. You'll benefit from that rhythm during the contracting conversations. This *Five-Year Marriage Basics: The Nitty Gritty* section gets more specific and is largely task-and-behavior-focused.

Hopefully, your past conversations helped you be more honest. And, when you argued, it wasn't the end of the world…or your relationship. Or, maybe it was…and if it was, you saved yourself years of heartache by finding out now what you would have found out later.

Be sure to **make enough time for effective contracting.** You can't wait until the week – or even the month – before the wedding to make agreements with each other. You have too many other things going on then. You need time to sort out the gems of your life and decide what you want now and what can wait until later. For a first marriage, it wouldn't be bad to begin as soon as you start talking seriously about marriage. For a subsequent marriage, it can be sometime in the year prior.

Also, when you have a Family Meeting, if your meeting is at noon on Sunday, you might feel like giving into the tendency to wait until Sunday morning to work on what you have both agreed to discuss. That won't be a good idea. I've done it and so has Joseph. When you do that, what happens is that you aren't prepared to talk about what *you* really *want*. The danger in doing it that way is that you will agree to something that isn't fully what you want.

Joseph and I usually give ourselves three months to work on the contracting process; we meet weekly. However, the last contracting was unlike the others. In the previous five years we had both experienced several life changes, including the unanticipated caregiving needs and subsequent deaths of both of our mothers, our last surviving parents. Those life changes gave us more to discuss. And, as I said to Joseph before we started, in our first marriage we felt like we had our whole life in front of us and all the time in the world. After twenty-five years, it wasn't the same case. We had to look at that reality. It impacted the content of our conversation. It was a very different contracting than when we were "new" together.

Because Joseph and I were facing some things that were, for us, uncharted territory, we started seven months in advance of our September wedding. We met twice a month during the spring and once a month during the summer. We didn't come to agreement until the end of August when we were on vacation.

Okay. You're almost ready.

Before you delve into *The Nitty Gritty* topics, review *The Beginnings* Ground Rules (time/place/agenda) and add these:

- **Do your homework.** Choose one area to discuss and give yourselves time to think about it alone before discussing it together.

  One way you can get your brain engaged in-between appointments is with the help of a notebook – one that you will only use for Family Meetings. Here's how to use it: At the top of a page, put the date of the next meeting and what you'll be discussing. Leave the notebook in a place where you will see it often. Two popular places (where you have time to think) are the car (say, on the seat beside you) or in the bathroom. Then, throughout the week, jot down some ideas. You'll be surprised at the ideas you can come up with while driving to or from work, while you're in the shower or brushing your teeth, or even when walking from the car to your workplace or into a store. When you keep the questions where you can see them, the best answers will bubble up from your unconscious into your conscious mind.

- **Be pleasant, patient, and open-minded.** It's easy to come to agreement when you're both in a good mood and feel safe. But some issues can push emotional buttons. So, when that happens, being kind will go a long way toward facilitating agreement.

- **Stay Positive.** If you don't reach agreement on something and the time is up, don't keep going around in a circle. Agree to bring that same point back at the next meeting. If you still can't reach agreement, that's a signal that you need outside help. Don't hesitate to get it.
  o If you decide to get help from someone outside the relationship (marriage counselor, marriage mediator), allow enough time for those appointments and follow-ups to happen, too.

- **Stay focused.** At the end of each meeting, choose one issue, or one or two specific points to think about between meetings that you'll discuss and negotiate at the next meeting. In-between meetings, each of you should be thinking and researching. Both of you need to be able to come to the next meeting with a few ideas, opinions, and choices for each subject you plan to discuss.

- **Be HONEST.** Ask any divorced person if s/he would have preferred knowing the truth at the beginning. Most will tell you they would, even if it was painful, inconvenient, or disappointing. The sting of finding out later (after a life together was started on shaky ground, or after children, or after too many angry things were said and self-esteem was damaged) was far greater.

- **Stick to the topic.** If you decide you're going to talk about how to handle money, don't veer off and talk about childcare (unless it's in the context of *paying* for childcare).

- **Be respectful of your partner.** Your contracting discussions should enable both of you to feel you are safe. That means that both of you need to void being condescending, demanding or bullying.
    - o If s/he doesn't see some relationship aspect, like saving money or staying faithful, as being as important as you do, that's significant. Give your partner the courtesy of listening to his/her point of view. Discuss it until you are both satisfied that you've been heard.
    - o Forcing your partner to agree to something isn't healthy. Moreover, it won't stick.
- **Agree to brainstorm.** Who knows what ideas you'll brainstorm together, but by brainstorming, you'll get something that's agreeable to both of you. If you reach an impasse and don't seem to be getting anywhere, put that topic to the side. Sometimes the seemingly biggest conundrums have a fairly simple solution, but one you can't see through your emotional glasses. Talk about it later or put it on a list to discuss with a marriage counselor or marriage mediator.

I know these seem like a lot of rules to remember and follow. But, as parameters, they will help you stay focused, on point...*and in love*.

Ready?

Shared Values

What are your *shared* values? You, and everyone else, live your life by what you value. If you aren't consciously clear about your values, you will have personal conflicts.

It's the same in a marriage. If you aren't consciously clear about what you value, as a couple and in your marriage, you *will* have conflicts.

Your core marriage values are what unite the two of you because they mutually guide your decisions and subsequent actions. You'll use your core values to figure out everything else. If you don't have shared values, you are likely to go in divergent directions.

For example, consider health as a top personal value. That value will color everything, from how you eat, your lifestyle, the kind of vacations you choose, and how you raise your kids. However, if "health" isn't a *shared* value, one of you will do something like making daily exercise a priority. That's good for one of you but likely to annoy your partner because s/he thinks you're wasting time and taking away from more important things.

What difference will shared values make?

Consider this: if God, honesty, financial security, health, and fun are your top shared values, you are likely to go to church services regularly, make plain speaking a house rule, build your savings, avoid debt, and choose a joint hobby that includes exercise and adventure (like hiking through all the major national parks).

However, if your shared values include family time, community involvement, balance, spirit, and teamwork, you are likely to make family dinners a priority, get involved in some kind of sports, join the Home and School Association or be involved in local politics, and focus your weekends on family outings or at-home events, like family movie night.

Can you see how those lifestyles are the results of values-driven decisions? Shared values will guide you and impact your everyday lifestyle.

In Chapter Four you started thinking about your personal values. Using those as a guide for discussion, start talking about your shared values with your partner.

- What are your personal top ten values? Think them through and then put them in order.
- Compare lists with your partner.
- What are the values you both share? Those values will shape how you live your life together.
- What are personal values that you don't share but agree to honor?

Pick the five values that you agree will guide you as a couple.

Name Change
Traditionally, a woman takes the name of the man she marries. However, it makes sense in the Five-Year Marriage for a woman to keep her own name and a man to keep his own name. But you may want to go a totally different route.

- Jay-Z (Shawn Carter) married Beyoncé Knowles and legally changed his name to Shawn Knowles-Carter
- John Lennon became John Winston Ono Lennon married to Yoko Ono Lennon
- Former Los Angeles mayor Antonio Villar married Corina Raigosa and combined their last names: Villaraigosa

Whatever you choose for *your* name, what about your children? Will a child's name be his, hers, a hyphenated name, or a combined version of both names? Decide together what last name your children will have.

Religion

For many couples, a specific spiritual practice (or lack of one) is either a curse or a blessing in a marriage. For the Five-Year Marriage couple, when it comes to religion, you can't just presume that your partner will "see it your way" sometime in the future. If religion or a specific spiritual philosophy is important to you, it will become an issue. If it isn't an issue before children come along, it will become one afterward.

Here are some of the questions you and your partner need to discuss:

- Did you grow up following a specific faith?
- Is it still important to you?
- Whether you practice it now or not, do you want religion to be part of your marriage?
- If you do, what would that look like for you?
  - Do you want your partner to embrace the same religion?
  - Will you attend weekly services?
  - What about your children? What religion will you want to raise them in?
  - Will you send your children to religious school?
- If you did not grow up with a specific faith, do you want to find one?
  - Why? What is it about a religious philosophy that is important for you *now*?
- If your partner isn't on the same page with religion, how will you handle it together?

Fidelity

One of the ideas with the Five-Year Marriage is that you and your partner are committed to each other for five years. It presumes your Five-Year Marriage includes a commitment of sexual faithfulness to each other. However, nobody is perfect and mistakes happen.

Infidelity hurts. So does indiscriminate sex that can result in STDs that affect a partner. You deserve to be and feel safe for the duration of your five-year commitment.

Also, infidelity usually requires premeditation. If one of you steps outside your marriage for sex, what is the significance and/or consequence?

What if one of you – or both of you – wants an open marriage or some other kind of sexual practice that is incongruent with fidelity? What does that mean for your Five-Year Marriage?

Whatever your sexual practices/desires are, the fidelity conversation is definitely one you'll want to have with each other.

Money
Before you start arguing over credit card bills or who should pay for what, figure out your priorities with money.
- What will your money priorities be as a couple?
    - It makes sense for you to pay your bills first. Right? Or do you disagree about that issue?
    - What about saving? Are you putting money aside for a house or your children's education?
    - How much money will you put into a "cushion" or "rainy day" fund?

- Where will you keep your money? Most traditional couples put everything in one shared account. However, in the Five-Year Marriage, you can easily do your finances differently.
    - Considering that your plan is to be together for five years, I suggest keeping your own accounts and have one shared checking account, one shared savings account and one house credit card. That enables you to keep enough of your own money to maintain your financial independence.
    - If you are a stay-at-home partner, how will the working partner enable you to do that? That is, how will the financial and childcare responsibilities work?
    - If one partner stays at home to raise children, what will be the other partner's responsibility to your joint financial well-being?

- o I also suggest that you both keep track of each other's accounts, particularly credit cards. You should both be aware of who owes what to whom.

- Download a copy of your credit reports
  - o Is there anything that you didn't know about your partner's finances? Is there anything that could negatively impact joint purchases, e.g. buying a house?
    - If there is, what can you do about it?
  - o Each of the three credit bureaus allows you to download your credit reports for free each year. So do it annually and check them – not only so you both know each other's finances but to make sure no one else has invaded your financial life.

- What's your FICO score? What's your partner's score?

- Looking at the credit report and your FICO scores, what do they tell each of you about you and your partner's attitude about money, credit, and financial responsibilities?

- How do you handle money? Do you spend everything and have huge credit card debt?
  - o Is one of you better at handling money?
  - o How will you pay bills?
    - Will one of you handle all the joint accounts while you each handle your individual bills?
    - Will one of you handle all the joint *and* personal bills?

- What about money tied to a previous relationship, e.g., are you paying child support? How will that money be handled?
- Do you have property that is not part of the relationship (e.g. business or an investment)?
  - o What will you do about that?
  - o If you keep the property separate, who will get that property if something happens to you or to the

marriage?

- Do you have property with children? How will you split that up, or will the children be the sole owners?

- How will you take title of the property you own together or will purchase together, as joint tenants or as tenants by the entirety?
  o How you take title to "real property" like houses or cars may be determined by how you want your assets to be divided and to whom they should go to in case of your untimely death.

- If you are getting life insurance, who will be the beneficiary and who will own the policy?
  o Being beneficiary and owner are two different things. Being each other's beneficiary may not be the most comprehensive way to have life insurance. Also, look into being the policy owner of each other's policies.
  o When deciding what you should do...
    ▪ Research and read about your options.
    ▪ See an attorney to find out how to protect yourself, your partner, and your children and/or heirs.

- Are you an emotional spender? That is, do you have emotional needs that you think money will solve? Examples of emotional spending would be "keeping up with the Joneses" spending, impulse buying, or an expensive hobby. On the other side of that coin, emotional needs could mean saving everything to the point of being miserly, cheap, or abusive.
  o Those are both extremes, but it could also be everything in between. What is it for the two of you?

Children
In the Five-Year Marriage, talking about children and their long-term care becomes a major issue. For some couples, it's the only real reason for getting married (versus living together). Yet, even when both

partners want children, I've seen marriages end because partners aren't honest about their feelings around having and raising their children.

Too often, in a traditional marriage, when it goes sour, children become the emotional football tossed back and forth between partners. Once-loving couples who are no longer together frequently vie for the attentions of the children. Some use money and power, others use permissiveness ("s/he lets me do it...why don't you?").

While most custody battles are private, ones that happen in public show how ugly child custody cases can become.

In 2007, actors Alec Baldwin and Kim Basinger fought over custody of their daughter, Ireland. When someone leaked a nasty voicemail to the press, it became worldwide news. Baldwin had to answer for calling his then-eleven-year-old daughter a "rude, thoughtless pig."

Jon and Kate Gosselin, of the reality television show *Jon and Kate Plus 8* (now *Kate Plus 8*), have been battling over their eight children for years. They've accused each other of a variety of sins. When Jon accused Kate of limiting his access to their children, he didn't just go through the courts. He went to *E! Online*.

Meanwhile, in a *Dr. Oz* appearance, Kate said, "Having an ex-husband who doesn't see the value in uplifting his children and his family, whether he chooses to be on the show or not, is extremely difficult. But I can't change those things. All I can change is me and my response and what I teach my children about it."[26]

Clearly, whether you already have children (with this partner or another one), or if one partner wants children and one doesn't (or any other scenario), the agreement you make about children will color how you live your Five-Year Marriage.

Whatever you and your partner decide, the children can never be pawns in the odd chess game of divorce. Figuring out how you will handle your children in advance will save them from being in the middle if you two decide not to continue together. Having a childcare agreement, one that you make while you are still "in love" with each other, is a form of love that will honor you and the children that will come your way as well as the children that are already part of your life. So, before you enter into the Five-Year Marriage, you need to decide about the children.

One benefit to the Five-Year Marriage is that you think through many of the issues around children in advance. If, when children arrive, your original agreements no longer work, you can renegotiate them.

Here are many of the points the two of you will need to discuss:
- Do you both want children?
- If you do, how many? How soon?
- If you are waiting, what kind of birth control will you use?
- Will one partner be a stay-at-home parent?
  - If not, how will you care for the children while you are both working?
- What will you do if you don't get pregnant? If you cannot have children in the traditional way:
  - Will you consider In Vitro Fertilization (IVF) or some other fertility treatment?
  - If you go the IVF route, how will you pay for it? For how long?
  - If you don't get pregnant with IVF, will you consider adoption? If so, will you consider only adopting domestically, or also internationally? How do you feel about transracial adoption?
  - If you don't ever have children, can you still have a happy life? That is, can you see yourself being "that special aunt" or coaching a team, or even starting a school, like Milton Hershey did with his spouse, Catherine?

One woman, Janet, told me that she and her spouse had an agreement that she would be a stay-at-home parent while he built his career. Janet gave up her career to raise their four children while he reached the top of his. Sadly, after twenty years, and just when Janet was starting to think about reviving her career, he decided to leave her for a younger woman. When I met Janet she was working at my fitness center cleaning equipment. She was lost, disillusioned, and bitter. Neither of you want that to happen, either to you or to your partner, right? So:

- If one partner is staying at home, that partner is in danger of losing whatever career equity s/he has earned. How will the working partner compensate the non-working partner for the loss of employment and career (see the "Money" section).

- Will the stay-at-home parent receive some specific and regular amount of money (that is not earmarked for the household, but just for that partner's use)?

- Will the stay-at-home parent have a fully funded IRA/Roth IRA?

- Will time and money accommodations be made so that the stay-at-home parent can stay connected to his/her career (e.g. through professional association meetings, maintaining licenses or credentials, continuing education classes and/or attendance at annual conferences)?

- How will the working partner cooperate in the care of the child/children?

- What experiences did you have growing up that you don't want to repeat with your own children? Some examples:
  - o Did you have an overbearing or unkind parent?
  - o Were your parents too harsh or too lenient?
  - o Did they get divorced, and you felt responsible?
  - o What do you need to do to spare your children that same feeling of guilt?

- When the children are old enough, how will you bring them into the discussion of the Five-Year Marriage? What age is "old enough" to you?

- If one or both of you have children from another relationship, what parameters will you agree on for those children?

When Steffie broke up with her college sweetheart, Joe, he met someone else right away. Joe's new girlfriend got pregnant and the couple married. The marriage was short-lived but Joe stayed in his daughter's life and took financial responsibility for her.

After a few years, when Steffie and Joe were both single, they met again. They married and had two children of their own. Joe continued to send money for his first child but each month Steffie begrudged the childcare money that was going to take care of her spouse's ex. In addition, Steffie felt resentment toward Joe's first child. It often resulted in arguments between Joe and Steffie and impacted their relationship.

- If that is your situation, how will you handle it differently than Joe and Steffie? You need to talk about it and come to an understanding.
  - ○ Remember, no child asks to be born. *You* make that choice. The child should never have to pay for your decision, even if it was a bad decision. If you hate the child's mother or father (who was previously with your partner), ***get over it***.
- If, after five years, you decide not to have another Five-Year Marriage, how will you agree to care for the child or children involved?
  - ○ Who will the child/children live with?
  - ○ What kind of financial arrangements will be made? For example, will there be a common account, specifically designated for childcare, into which one or both partners will contribute?
    - If there is a disparity in incomes, instead of a dollar amount, what percentage of each partner's salary will go into a common account for the care and feeding of children?

NOTE: There is more about children and the effect of the Five-Year Marriage in the next chapter.

Shared Responsibility

A relationship takes work, and not just the emotional part. You live someplace, and that place has to be taken care of by someone. Who will that be?

Even if you hire people to do chores, like cleaning your house, someone has to be responsible for hiring, firing, and paying that person. Who will do that in your partnership?

Remember, if you sign on for a chore, you are committed to doing it. You can always renegotiate, revise, and amend your agreement. You can do that through Family Meetings. You might not feel the need to do that for years – or ever. However, reconfiguring your shared responsibilities is something that can be on the table at the end of five years.

So, *while you are in negotiations*, what chores are yours? Here are some common household chores and some suggestions:

- **Monthly finances.** This includes paying bills, keeping track of savings, and monitoring investments, including your IRA. If one partner does all the detail work, how can the other partner participate so that all the responsibility for bills isn't on one partner? Maybe that partner can complete a monthly update of your financial picture, or check credit card statements to make sure returns are credited, and shred whatever needs it. You should have some way for both partners to know where your family stands financially.

- **Cleaning.** In several Five-Year Marriages, Joseph and I did all the house cleaning. We don't clean the same way and we don't make the bed the same way. Seemingly insignificant things like that bothered me. My solution was that one week I cleaned the first floor and he cleaned the second. The following week we switched. If something wasn't done the way I wanted it, I knew it would be "my way" the following week. It saved us a ton of arguments!

- **Yardwork.** This includes lawn mowing, planting annuals and perennials, etc. It's anything that needs to be done to the lawn, either for maintenance or beauty. You can split this up. One partner might be better at maintenance and the other better at the aesthetics.

- **Laundry.** Do your own. For joint laundry, decide who will be responsible for sheets and towels and children's clothing. You can share those; for example, if one of you does the washing and drying, the other one can do the folding.

- **Car Maintenance.** Again, do your own.

- **Meals**
  - **Cooking.** Who is good at it? Who gets home early enough to make dinner? Does it work for you to cook the week's meals on a weekend? What about lunches, including lunches for children?

  - **The Family Dinner.** How meaningful is it to gather around the table with your partner and, in time, your whole family?

    Family dinner is where you learn to laugh, argue, tease, share, and love each other. Many families never miss a night. In fact, it's the only time some parents find out how their children think and feel about what's happening in their lives. It's when they get to have actual conversations. Some families have even started having "device-free" dinners – no phones, no tablets, nothing but food and conversation at the dinner table.

    For some who grew up with family dinners, *and those who wish they had*, having a meal together each night is crucial to the family dynamic. Maybe you can't do it every night, but you can make a rule that you have to eat dinner together as a family (even if it's a family of two) at least four nights a week. Or you could decide that family dinner on Sunday is "mandatory."

Many viewers of television shows like *Blue Bloods* and *Duck Dynasty* admit that the family dinner is their favorite part. In those shows, like in real life, everyone goes their separate ways by day, but the intergenerational dinner gathering brings them together. And, in both of those television families, they begin the meal with a prayer or an expression of gratitude. Many real life families do too!

What about you? If the family dinner is important to one of you but not the other, that can cause some disappointments or even serious arguments.

- **Social Activities**. One partner or another may be more social or have more business activities that require a social component. How will you handle that? How will the less social partner balance out the efforts of the more social partner?
  - o Make a list of things you both like to do together. They can be anything social, like going to the movies, seeing a show or concert, having a picnic at a local park, or anything else. If you want to do something nice for your partner, you can look at the list.

  - o We almost always give our spouses clues. So *listen to what s/he says*. If s/he says, "I'd love to [go to a certain game or watch a certain team, see a certain performer…whatever]," then find out if s/he is serious about wanting it and, if s/he is, then figure out a way to make it happen.

  - o *If you are the less social person*, one thing you can do to create a feeling of reciprocity for the more social partner is to figure out what you can do just for that partner.

- *If you are the more social partner*, make a list of things of the things you like doing, including plays, movies, museums, going down the shore for a day, and anything else you enjoy. That will help your less-social partner get ideas. Also, you know, s/he is not a mind-reader, so if you know something is coming up, suggest it.

Since I'm the more social partner, I usually schedule the majority of our social activities. That was fine during out first marriages. However, by Marriage#3, I became annoyed that I was doing too much "work" for our social life and Joseph wasn't.

So, for Christmas, I began asking for just one thing, the same thing, every year: a monthly "event" that Joseph plans for me. It doesn't have to be something big and the cost can come from the house funds. But it has to be something I want to do and he has to do all the planning.

For example, I'm not a football fan. If Joseph got me tickets to a Philadelphia Eagles game (he's an avid fan) I'd give my ticket away.

On the other hand, I'm a passionate Philadelphia Phillies fan, and I love fireworks. Each year Joseph makes a point to get tickets to the Philadelphia Phillies for a night when they have fireworks after the game (fireworks are one of my all-time favorite things to see). He invites my favorite cousins and we make a night of it.

The game with fireworks is a great night, not just because I love baseball and the Phils, fireworks, and my cousins, but because I know Joseph put time and effort into making that night special for me.

- **Miscellaneous tasks.** These are things that happen *sometimes*, like hiring a contractor or taking a trip. Somebody has to make that happen, and the responsibility shouldn't fall on one person. For example, figure out who can do the research before you make a purchase (which one of you loves doing research?) or where to go and what to do on your next vacation (who is better at planning?).

Of course, these are not *all* the possibilities for shared responsibilities (see more in the "Family Obligations" section), but they encompass most of the big ones. If you sort these out, and make agreements about them, you'll have a good head start. Others will come up along the way. When something does, and it's clear that the task is going to be a recurring event (versus a one-off), make an agreement about it.

Family Obligations

What obligations do you have toward your children from other relationships or your parents or other family members?

- **In-laws and friends.** These two groups of people are usually really important to each partner. If you don't get along with a future in-law or a close friend, how will you and your partner handle it? In the sitcom, *Modern Family*, Jay resents that his son-in-law, Phil, eloped with daughter Claire and that he didn't get a chance to walk his daughter down the aisle. Phil goes out of his way to get Jay's approval and Claire works really hard at making sure her father doesn't make life too hard for Phil.
  - o Do you have a similar situation?
  - o What arrangement can you both make to ensure that each of you has enough time with your family and friends while still honoring your partnership time?
    - Will you split holidays between families, take turns hosting the families or do something else?
  - o What agreement can you two make about in-laws or friends that will lessen the tension between you and your partner?

My family always celebrated the holidays – Christmas, Easter, Memorial Day, July 4th, Labor Day, Mother's Day, Father's Day and birthdays. Joseph's family didn't celebrate most of those. However, to his mother, Christmas, Mother's Day and her birthday were especially important.

In our first marriage, we would have Christmas Eve with one family and Christmas with the other. And switch it around the next year (both mothers lived close enough to do that easily).

Mother's Day was another story. We tried hosting Mother's Day at our house with both mothers. First we tried a family dinner, then a brunch, but neither worked out very well for the moms.

So, one year, Joseph and I split for Mother's Day. It worked out well. From that year forward, Joseph spent the day with his family, either to his sister's house or out to dinner with his mother. While he did that, I went with my mom. Sometimes we went to my sibling's house. Then, for several years, it was a day for just my mother and me, often to Atlantic City and the casinos.

In later years, when my mother-in-law was in a nursing home, we would have an early meal with her and a later meal with my mother (or vice versa).

- **More about your in-laws and friends.** How will you handle invitations (extending them or accepting them), buying gifts, sending birthday cards, etc.? Will one of you do it or will you each take care of the relationship maintenance with your own parents, siblings, and other relatives?

- **Caregiving.** Are there certain people whose care needs to be addressed?
  o Will you have your children from a past relationship with you for holidays, vacations, and/or weekends?
    ▪ How will you handle it?
    ▪ How will you tell others (your family, your children) to handle it?
  o Are you responsible for a parent's care, either in your home or financially?
  o During this Five-Year Marriage, what impact do you foresee caregiving having on your life together?

Emotional Support

Emotional support is something that makes you feel that people care. It can lift you up, help you through a tough patch and even boost your confidence. Emotional needs vary from person to person. Also, they shift and change with time. So you will want to have a conversation about emotional support on an annual basis. However, for your current discussions and current Five-Year Marriage, based on what you know about yourself, what kind of emotional support do you require from your partner? Some examples include:

- Words. One of you might need to hear things like, "I love you" or "I'm really glad we are together" or "You did the right thing" or some other emotional assurance on a regular basis.
- Physical connection: Holding hands, snuggling or cuddling.
- Getting a pat on the back accompanied with "nice job."
- Being acknowledged, e.g. when you are come home from work or when you walk into a room (vs. being unobserved, unnoticed or ignored).
  o Scheduling enough time for relationship maintenance, e.g., a weekly date, a movie night, intimacy, or something else. Plan on doing it on a regular basis. What is "regular" for you? Discuss and decide together.
  o Private time – for hobbies, sports, classes, friend time, or whatever is meaningful to each of you. NOTE: this might change sooner than in five years if you have children. You can talk about that now, or bring it up in a Family Meeting in the months before the baby is born.
  o Romance. Let your partner know what your emotional needs for romance are. Does romance mean a date night out, a quiet dinner for two, sex, or something else?

Boundaries
- Boundaries are the way of separating your thoughts and feelings from that of your partner, family, friends, children, and others. It's how you keep your SELF intact. It's also how you prevent succumbing to overcare and getting so sucked into someone else's bubble that you no longer know where you end and the other person begins.

  Setting boundaries start with looking at how you feel, figuring out what makes you feel good and/or empowered, and what doesn't. Boundaries will establish what you will, as partners, accept and allow between yourselves...*and what you won't*. They can cover every area from private time to money to sex. Sample boundaries:

- o "I only want civil conversation. I'm happy to talk with you as long as our conversation maintains a civil tone. We won't call each other names and there can't be any abusive or foul language."
- o "You are not allowed to use me as your emotional punching bag."
- o "My job is not to fix everything for everyone else. I can support others in fixing their own problems, but I'm not the fixer."
- o The 24-hour rule: "I will do what I can to help you, but you *must* give me a twenty-four hour window so I can figure out my time. If you don't give me twenty-four hours, expect me to say 'no'."
- o I expect you to honor my "me" time. That includes when I'm taking a shower, using the bathroom, out for a walk or at the gym, or when out with my friends.

*One of my personal boundaries is that no one is allowed to yell at me. That doesn't mean Joseph and I don't raise our voices when we argue; we do (and loudly) in a **two-sided** disagreement. But for anyone to just yell at me, that's simply not acceptable. No one, including Joseph, is allowed to yell at me. It's that simple. **No one**.*

Some of these boundaries are your personal ones and include not only your partner and children, but also everyone in your life. Other boundaries may be for just these five years. For instance, you might have a boundary specific to some of your partner's family or friends ("I'm not sending your family birthday cards"). Over time, your relationship might change (your sister-in-law has become your friend) and that boundary is no longer necessary or appropriate.

At the same time, what if your partner has a boundary that says, "I don't want you to look at my texts or look at who has called me." Are you okay with that? If you are, great. If you aren't, you need to discuss it.

Being clear about your boundaries is fair to your partner. Staying true to your boundaries is fair to you. That means if you say, for example, that you have a 24-hour rule, but give in each time you're asked to do something at the last minute, *you don't have a 24-hour rule*. If you say it's important to you, but then don't honor it yourself, it's confusing to everyone else.

Once you talk about these matters, and you are good with each other's boundaries, you will have developed a clearer picture of what your Five-Year Marriage will look like.

Conflicts

No matter how much in love you are with each other, conflicts will surface. Conflict is normal and can even be good. Your partner may have reasons why s/he is in conflict with some aspect of your life together.

When conflicts happen, what will you do about them?

In any marriage, it's important to know *how* you argue. Do you have an argument style? It can take some couples years to figure each other's arguing style. And, by then, there could be long-term damage. So, understanding that you *are* going to argue, then thinking and discussing your arguing style *now* can help you avoid damage later.

What do you do in an argument?

- Do you keep things in and seem OK with everything but are simmering on the inside? And then one thing sets you off and you blow up?
- Are you defensive? Do you take offense at every comment and feel like you have to defend yourself?
- Will you do or say anything (even if it's not true) just to avoid an argument?

- Are you passive? Do you clam up and let your louder or more persistent partner undermine your argument, opinion, or feelings? Then, you sulk for day or get resentful or passive aggressive?
- Are you the partner who is louder and gets excited or angry faster? Does that feel dominating or bullying to your partner?
- Do you want to stay and argue even when you are both going around in circles?
- Do you leave [the room, the house, the situation] when you experience conflict?

What can you do to handle conflict better? Here are a couple of techniques that could help:
- Write out your thoughts and feelings. When you write those down in advance, you are less likely to forget what you want to say when the emotions of the subsequent discussion make you forget. The written-down words will be there remind you.
- Clearly define the problem and then keep the argument focused on solutions.
- Focus on behaviors instead of personality.
- Decide if cursing or bad-mouthing is out of the question (either one of those can escalate an argument another level or two).
- In the middle of an argument, if it gets heated, take a "cool-down" break.

If you want to get some insight through an assessment, try the one in *Psychology Today Magazine*:[28]

Deal Breakers
In the Five-Year Marriage, you promise to be together for five years. You agree that you will stay together and work to build your love and solve problems together. But the Five-Year Marriage isn't "for better or for worse." Some behaviors aren't worth the effort needed for keeping a relationship together.

Just in case one of you isn't clear about what not being "for better or for worse" means, here are some "deal-breakers" in your Five-Year Marriage:

- Infidelity (unless you have an open marriage or some other kind of mutual agreement)
- Abuse: domestic abuse, domestic violence, emotional abuse, sexual abuse, or exploitation
- Financial misuse or corruption: This includes one partner controlling the money, or running up debt on undisclosed credit cards or forging a partner's signature for a purchase you both haven't agreed to make (like a boat, second house, etc.)
- Addiction

What is a deal-breaker for you?

Everyone has unique deal-breakers. And with each deal-breaker, there is a reason why one thing or another is more than one partner wants to deal with in marriage.

When I was growing up, my father never drank. However, when I was a teenager, he was advised by his physician to have a drink at night. Long story short, one drink became many and he became an alcoholic. I watched alcohol turn an exceptionally good man into someone unrecognizable.

Anyone who has ever lived with an alcoholic knows it's bad. Alcoholism, like any addiction, devastates families. As a result, I knew I'd never want to repeat that experience. Alcoholism is a deal-breaker for me in any relationship.

You and your partner need to name and discuss the deal-breakers and the reasons for them. You both need to be perfectly clear about what your marriage is and what it isn't. Any negative behavior can be a deal-breaker, but you have to name them, be specific about how the behavior is negative and agree on the consequences, *before* you start your Five-Year Marriage (particularly if children are involved). Clarity is key!

Warning: if someone has a long list of deal-breakers, s/he can be using the process to a gain excessive power and control that results in domestic abuse. Be aware!

Five Years Means Five Years
The Five-Year Marriage is designed to give you a full five years together. At the end of five years, you can continue your contract as it is, adjust or revise your current contract or split up (the same as a divorce). However, in the meantime, you commit to the agreements you made in this contract and, as necessary, develop your problem-solving skills.

There is a good reason for doing your Five-Year Marriage this way.

Many couples will tell you that problems often arise in the middle of that time (e.g., three or seven years) and can sometimes end a marriage. Staying together through that time and working a problem out can be the difference between growing together and becoming more intimate or becoming resentful and getting a divorce.

As one divorced friend told me years after her four-year marriage ended, "We just didn't know what else to do, so we split up. Looking back, I can see now it was something we could have worked out. We just didn't know how."

Not knowing how to fix a problem is one reason for a high divorce rate. The other is that many couples – or sometimes just him or her – ignore a problem and think it will work itself out over time. When it doesn't, the problem festers. Then, by the time the couple actually go for counseling, it's a "last ditch effort" to fix a long-standing problem. But, by then, much more hurt and resentment has probably built up between the once-loving couple. When so much pain has occurred, it's much harder to salvage the relationship. It's not impossible, but it takes so much more time and effort to get back on track.

Because of your Five-Year Marriage, motivation is on your side. If you have problems, you know how much time is left to get help. Since you know the clock is ticking, you have the motivation to take action.

If, at the end of five years, you can't or don't want to keep going – then there's nothing to renegotiate. You end the marriage.

Presuming you're married with a standard marriage license, you will get a standard divorce. The Five-Year Marriage agreements you make at the beginning will help you end your marriage without some of the devastating acrimony that destroys many people during the divorce.

Wrap Up
Don't forget, with all the work you are doing, keep your Five-Year Marriage agreements in a single place, like a Five-Year Marriage couple's journal (separate from your personal journal or file). When you have a Family Meeting, review those agreements. You'll need to do that because, even with good faith and especially for the first year, one or both of you will forget. It won't be on purpose, but habits are hard to change. If you keep your Five-Year Marriage agreements in one place, and where you both can find them easily, you are more likely to keep the agreements. The reminder will be refreshing to your relationship.

Finally, how often can you and your partner have a Five-Year Marriage reality check? You can have them once a week, once a month, or twice a year – whatever serves your Five-Year Marriage.

In my family, Joseph and I call *our* reality checks the "Family Meeting." Sometimes we have one every other week, and we might do that for months (usually when we are working on a goal or a specific issue). Then we can go for months without one – until something big happens and we realize our partnership is getting off track. We make a plan to start the meetings up again.

You'll need to schedule your Family Meetings the same way you would schedule any important business meeting or medical appointment. And, just like you do your health-related "regulars" with an annual mammogram, physical, and dental cleaning, you need to plan for *at least* two meetings a year.

NOTE: Ad-hoc discussions while you're driving someplace aren't the same as scheduled appointments.

Having a Family Meeting and keeping your Five-Year Marriage contract and agreements handy will help you decide what you need or want to change before your next Five-Year Marriage.

More about Family Meetings in Chapter Six, *"Behind Closed Doors: Living the Five-Year Marriage."*

You will find a template for creating your Five-Year Marriage Contract in the RESOURCES section.

Chapter Five: Joseph's Take

I wasn't really into doing Family Meetings when we first started them. I felt then that I'd much rather be watching a Saturday Penn State football game or the Philadelphia Eagles on a Sunday afternoon or a Monday night.

It didn't take long to figure out that the Family Meetings were extremely helpful and an important part of our relationship. I like that the Family Meetings give Annmarie and I a regular place to air out and discuss our differences. And, if something comes up during the week and I don't want to discuss it then (Annmarie has a way of bringing things up while we're driving someplace), I simply suggest that we put it into the next Family Meeting. If one isn't scheduled we plan one.

That works great for me. Instead of feeling like I'm on the spot, I can table a discussion for after I have time to think about the subject. Over the years it saved a lot of the kind of arguments that used to happen when I wasn't ready to talk about something and felt pressured. At least now, if Annmarie and I argue, we both have our opinions thought out.

I say the benefits of Family Meetings outweigh the disadvantages.

Chapter Six
Behind Closed Doors:
Living the Five-Year Marriage

Chains do not hold a marriage together.
It is threads, hundreds of tiny threads,
which sew people together through the years.
Simone Signoret, Actress

The wedding is over. The honeymoon was wonderful. Now you can begin living the marriage that you so thoughtfully and lovingly created. What bliss, eh?

Wait! You say you had an argument? You say it started with money and, before you knew it, you were arguing about your mother-in-law. Then s/he walked out in the middle of it? When s/he came home, nothing got resolved. You weren't talking and you went to bed angry. You felt alone for the first time since the wedding. It didn't feel good.

Then, last week you went to dinner, and s/he was texting friends. Was s/he ignoring you? You found yourself thinking that you could have stayed home, saved the money, and watched television while you ate. You would have enjoyed dinner more.

How did that happen?

After all, you both spent so much time working out your explicit Five-Year Marriage contract; your marriage should be running smoothly, right?

Wrong!

Logically, just like in a traditional marriage, you started out wanting the fairy tale. So, at first, you tolerated little sidetracks and omissions. You hoped they were aberrations, just an unintentional misstep by the person with whom you share your life.

But before long, you realize she is *no* fairy tale princess and he is *not* Prince Charming.

That's when you wake up to the truth, to life. Errors in judgment happen; hurtful words are spoken, even shouted. You find yourself totally surprised *because you didn't even know* you could get *that* angry with *anybody* – ever. So how could you possibly be *that angry* with the person you love more than anyone else?

It happens.

Your Five-Year Marriage, just like life itself, won't always run smoothly. To think that it would, or could, is simply not a realistic expectation.

What *is* realistic is to *recognize* what the true heart and soul of your Five-Year Marriage really is. Once you do, then be willing and able to embrace its essence.

What *is* that essence?

Agreements. *Your own Five-Year Marriage agreements*, the ones you talked about and agreed to for your joint purpose, goals, responsibilities and more.

In case you haven't figured it out yet, *every* relationship is comprised of agreements. That's what people do, whether they say it or not. It doesn't matter if the relationship is with a person, company, or group. The agreement might be spoken or assumed. Either way, there's no getting around it. If you are *in a relationship*, you *have* an agreement, a social contract. It's how life is.

Remember that deal you made with your cell phone carrier or your cable company? Through that arrangement, the company agrees to provide a service, and you agree to pay your bills.

As long as you are doing your part, you have the reasonable expectation of reliable service, right? Yet in the real world, that doesn't always happen, does it? Sometimes, *even when you are paying your bill on time*, there is an interruption of service. Sometimes it's because there's a storm and your cable goes out. Or your phone dies. It happens.

What do you do? You contact your provider because you know your contract spells out who's supposed to do what, and what happens if something goes wrong.

In addition, you know when your contract is up. When that time is approaching, you decide if you're satisfied with the service and renew. Or you choose to renegotiate and get a better deal. Sometimes you choose to terminate the contract and look for something better.

It's the same with your Five-Year Marriage. It isn't designed to prevent all the problems between partners. It doesn't eliminate all the obstacles. The Five-Year Marriage contract is designed to give you a solid track to run on and a reason for running.

However, it isn't a stagnant or sluggish agreement. It's ever-active and dynamic. And, just like any track, it has hurdles and stumbling stones. For instance, as you live day-by-day in your Five-Year Marriage, you'll discover that few people will be able to push your buttons like that person with whom you share your daily life.

Just like your cell or cable service, something can go awry when there is some kind of disruption or disturbance. In that respect, your Five-Year Marriage won't be unlike a traditional marriage.

What *will* be different is this: In a traditional marriage most of the really important agreements are unsaid and often presumed. You may have recognized that kind of agreement between your parents. If you think about it, you can probably come up with few of their implied agreements. In fact, you probably joke about them with your siblings, like "Remember how we knew when Mom wanted Dad to do something because she'd cook his favorite meal?" Or, "You always knew when Dad was in the doghouse because he'd bring home some flowers for Mom."

Of course, that's a simplistic and non-threatening example, *but you noticed*, right? You noticed other things too, *right*?

As an adult, you're likely to mirror what you saw in your parents' relationships. If your parents had a good relationship, then you perceive the agreements of marriage to be easy, doable, and amicable.

On the other hand, some parents had arrangements that weren't as cordial and agreeable. Some of them were one-sided understandings that resulted in constant arguing or resentments. They might have involved things like harshness, infidelity, abuse, neglect, distance, or some other unpleasant behavior. Maybe you wondered how your mother put up with your father's behavior or how your father tolerated your mother's cold ways. If you asked, maybe s/he said something like, "It doesn't bother me. That's just how s/he is."

It might not have bothered your mother or father, but it bothered you. Now, as you think about your own relationship, it isn't what you want.

Still, you start to notice something happening in your Five-Year Marriage. Those "mom or dad behaviors" you're noticing didn't show up before the wedding. Maybe they didn't even show up in the first year. However, as life happens around and between you and your spouse, some of those behaviors are very likely to surface sometime during your Five-Year Marriage. Like it or not, whether your parents had a good, rocky, or failed marriage, that was your norm. When those behaviors pop up, recognize them for what they are: you're mirroring the actions of the parent or parents that were your primary role models.

When that happens, think about the kind of agreement(s) your parents had. The parental agreements of your childhood can affect your Five-Year Marriage.

Maybe disruptive patterns weren't with your parents, but in your previous marriage or relationship. You ask yourself, "How is this happening *again*?" The answer might be in questioning what kind of unspoken reasoning could be creating the same situation for you.

What do you do? Can you prevent it? Can you two change course?

Yes! If you pay attention and are willing to do what it takes now, before those damaging patterns get set in stone.

Something else that shows up while you're living the Five-Year Marriage: a change of mind. Let's say you figured you would both focus on your careers. Now one of you wants to have children. Maybe you've even mentioned it to your partner and presumed s/he understood and would be receptive to the change. S/he wasn't. Now what?

Look to your Five-Year Marriage Contract. Why did you decide to wait to have children? Is that reason still valid? If it is, then stick to your agreement. Of course, if things have changed and that original reason no longer holds water – and you *both* recognize and agree to it – you can make a change to your original deal. Life happens and something can create dramatic shifts. You could have a serious medical problem or you could win the lottery. Good and bad things can happen.

However, if your reason is because all your friends are talking about their biological clocks and are having babies, so now you want one, that reasoning doesn't hold water. You can't use your biological clock as a reason. You knew your ages when you made the agreement. That wouldn't change, so that cause alone wouldn't be a good reason. Something else would have to happen to make the biological clock case make sense in order to change the timing in your original agreement.

What if you think your partner is having second thoughts about having children at all? Maybe you decided you wanted to start having children in the first year of your *next* Five-Year Marriage. Then her business takes off and she doesn't seem interested. That could be a deal-breaker for you.

Changing your agreement can't happen just because one of you suddenly decides on a whim that you want it to switch. You made an agreement and have a plan based on that agreement.

That's what the Five-Year Marriage is all about, that's how and why it works better and more effectively than traditional marriages. With the Five-Year Marriage you agree on specifics, like your vision, purpose, goals, and your shared responsibilities – and you say them out loud. They become the gauges, benchmarks, and boundaries that you both agree to follow. The Five-Year Marriage contract becomes the blueprint for your partnership. It's a practical guide for your day-to-day living.

That's not to say that you can't set standards and principles in a traditional marriage. You can. Many couples do. Then things get busy and life happens; couples often forget about them. That's because there is no system, structure, or end-date that keeps couples on track.

That's one of the beauties of the Five-Year Marriage. You design the partnership you call your Five-Year Marriage and keep track of it. As life and people change, your Five-Year Marriage acknowledges the changes. Your Five-Year Marriage allows you the mental and emotional agility to make modifications with a timeframe in which to do it.

Your Five-Year Marriage contract does not presume perfection any more than traditional marriage does. The major difference between living a Five-Year Marriage instead of a traditional marriage is that the timed end-date for your current marriage gives you a *compelling* reason to pay attention to and evaluate your relationship, as partners. So, when you have a problem, there's no slack time to act like traditional couples in marriage (which often means living in denial for a long time).

By contrast, traditional couples think they have the luxury of forced longevity in their "forever" marriage. When problems surface, it doesn't matter if the couple is twenty or fifty; many choose "safe excuses" as the reason for their problems. They may argue about the same issue, over and over again, but not resolve anything. When they don't settle disagreements, they push away that ominous internal dialogue in favor of hoping time alone will resolve differences. The anger, hurt, and resentment is often ignored. Instead of getting better, it aggravates, worsens, and estranges.

Over time, the majority of traditional couples sleepwalk through their marriage, focusing instead on career, children, and domestic matters. Sometimes the partnership of spouses is replaced with the sanctuary of close family or friends, social media, clandestine affairs, and even internet porn. They allow those distractions to bring a false feeling of excitement or security to their individual lives.

By the time the traditional couple gets to year four or five, they often have a serious problem. By then the relationship can be tense and painful or worse – indifferent. When they try figuring out where things got off-track, the conversation brings up more anger, blame, and resentment than understanding, forgiveness, and resolution. Years can go by before the couple is ready to admit there is a serious problem. By then, one or both spouses may start wondering if the relationship is even salvageable. If they aren't talking about divorce, they're probably thinking about it.

If they want to stay together, the couple needs to make a major commitment of time and energy and may even need therapy to bring the marriage back to life. If not, they become two people sharing a house but going their separate ways.

That's not for you.

Still, if you don't take care of the business of your relationship from the get-go, after five years, there may be no relationship needing your care.

During the beginning of the contracting process (Chapter Four, *Five-Year Marriage Basics: The Beginnings*) you and your prospective spouse articulated what you wanted from your Five-Year Marriage. Next, you clarified your goals and expectations (Chapter Five, *Five-Year Marriage Basics: The Nitty Gritty*). Presuming you were honest and open with your feelings and agreements, you established a "norm." You designed the "standards" that will guide your relationship. You drafted your agreement. Those heartfelt discussions facilitated more communication than the average couple has in five years – *or ever*! All that work will, in the future, enable you to better share feelings and concerns as things come up.

Still, maybe not right away, but at some point, you notice detours you weren't expecting. You get nervous, or scared, and wonder what's going wrong.

That's when, as you live life through your Five-Year Marriage, you need to remind yourselves that (1) you are equal partners in the relationship, and (2) you have an agreement you can both reference before you get stuck or hateful, and (3) you know there is not enough time for unresolved feelings to continue for very long. If you are giving your Five-Year Marriage attention, you're evaluating your contract and agreements through conversations and your Family Meeting.

How do you discuss your Five-Year Marriage? What do you talk about?

Here are Six Keys to keeping your Five-Year Marriage up to speed:
Mind the Store
Follow the Ground Rules
Turn the Communication Key
Remember Your Purpose
Make Magic with Habits
Make the Most of Your Family Meetings

Admittedly, it takes effort to remember to do these at the beginning of your marriage. Sometimes it doesn't seem necessary and, after all, you're both busy. When will you find the time?

Those are excuses. If you want to make excuses for not taking care of your relationship, then don't have a Five-Year Marriage. Keep this in mind: if you don't *find time* for your marriage, you'll be *making time* for divorce.

However, if you are serious about your Five-Year Marriage, these six ideas will become part of your family routine. When you do them from the beginning, they become a normal part of what you do. They will be habits…good habits. Later on, when life starts getting in the way or children come along, these will already be part of your relationship routine. They'll already be in your Five-Year Marriage arsenal.

Mind the Store
Have you ever baked your favorite treat and, as you start to add ingredients, you remember that you ran out of sugar the last time you baked something? Then you forgot to put it on the shopping list and now you're stuck. Ticked off, you ask yourself, "Why didn't I put it on my shopping list or make a note on my phone or something?" Now you either have to go to the store or take a chance and just leave it out of the mix and hope nobody notices. You don't really like either of those options.

Okay, maybe it's not sugar. It could be a file, credit card bill, drill bit, pantyhose…anything.

The point is that you need to take inventory and keep track of what you have. If you don't, you won't know when you're missing something that you'll need sooner or later. Then, when you want or need that "sugar" – or whatever – it won't be there for you.

It's the same when you're living the Five-Year Marriage.

You can't wait until the end of "year five" of your Five-Year Marriage to take inventory. You don't *suddenly* notice that you don't feel like you're a priority in your relationship or that you aren't getting what you need to feel good in your relationship. It's been creeping into your consciousness over time but you weren't naming and claiming it.

You need to pay attention *regularly* to how you feel. You have to do it in year one, two, three, and four. If you don't, you get stuck and, after a while, you lose out.

Similarly, you can't wait until the end of five years to notice the ***good*** things. If your partner does something that supports you or makes you feel good, you have to let him or her know about it. It doesn't matter if you tell everyone else. If s/he doesn't hear it directly from you, it won't count.

In the Five-Year Marriage, you *cannot* take anything for granted…the good or the bad. *That's especially true about the good stuff.*

That's what happens in a lot of traditional marriages. One person *presumes* their partner "just knows" that you love them or you appreciate what s/he does. Unfortunately, that's often not the case. Also, when s/he misses an opening for saying something nice, s/he decides it's okay because, after all, s/he has "forever" to make up for the missed opportunity.

Frankly, that's a losing practice for everyone involved. It's the baking equivalent of pretending that putting a lot of icing on top of a cake will make up for the missing sugar in the batter.

Of course, for any couple, those missed moments matter. However, for the couple who chooses the Five-Year Marriage it's even more important because you aren't living on "traditional marriage time." You have a time limit, a closing date.

So remember to mind the store by taking inventory regularly and replenishing what's needed, *before the next time you need it.* A simple "Thank you for coming with me to [some event] even though you knew you'd be bored" will go a long way in adding some sugar to a challenging time. Or you can praise a special behavior, "You know, when you did [x], it made me feel really good." And there's always the personality reminder, "One of the things I always liked about you was that you could make me laugh. You still do." Anything like that brings your spouse back to a time when you liked everything about each other. All of them can add sweetness to the mix before all the sugar runs out. Plus, in a challenging time, a little sugar can throw open emotional doors that are starting to close.

In Marriage#3 of my Five-Year Marriage, I was feeling like I wasn't the most important person in Joseph's life. One afternoon I was working on my business with a coach. Somehow my marriage came up. I didn't realize that I'd set off a warning bell, but the coach did. We talked about it briefly. At the end of the session, she gave me an "assignment" to write "Ten Things that Make Annmarie Feel Special." That seemed reasonable. What surprised me was how hard it was to make up that list.

However, just the process of doing it, of making myself choose and then articulating those ten things to myself, made a big difference. It made a difference in my level of expectation. It also validated and boosted feelings of deservedness and self-worth. Even if I would never have shared that list with Joseph, it was a good exercise for me. But, of course, I shared it with Joseph. Then I asked him to do the same. Joseph did and shared his list with me. It was helpful to both of us during that marriage. It continues to help us, from one marriage to the next, to form healthy partner-appreciation habits.

If you let things go, by the end of five years, you'll be long out of sugar. And it may be too late to replenish it. Not that you couldn't try, but it'll be a lot harder to find sweetness in a languishing relationship.

That doesn't mean, in your Five-Year Marriage, that you keep a ledger. However, it *does* mean that, as you go through your Five-Year Marriage, you pay attention and keep track of what's working and what's not.

To effectively "mind the store" while living your Five-Year Marriage, you have to make time for it. That means you must keep your Five-Year Marriage agreements close at hand and talk about them from time to time. You want to honor each other's requests (e.g., the "what makes me feel special" list). Your marriage won't thrive if you ignore the problems that come up or overlook each other's needs.

In addition, just like most *stores* have regular inventory reviews and meetings, *your marriage* can do the same thing (with Family Meetings). When you make the time and effort to address problems as you go along, three good things happen:

1 – You get used to sharing your grievances and learn to respect each other's feelings faster. Yes, it's true that nobody likes being told they aren't doing something right. Yes, that can cause some disagreement. Also, asking someone to change a behavior doesn't mean s/he will, or will do it fast or easily. However, if you can explain why something hurts your feelings or makes you crazy, your partner is more likely to understand and make the effort to accommodate your needs.

2 – Presuming you aren't unreasonable in your requests and don't expect your partner to be perfect, you two will develop a satisfying way to meet each other's needs. If you cannot, you will know – sooner rather than later – to get outside help. It will also help you decide if you want another Five-Year Marriage.

3 – If you acknowledge problems *before* you have a huge argument, and before anger and resentments build up, you are less likely to wait until something gets "big" to unload all the dirty laundry in your relationship basket.

Regular Family Meetings are a good way to mind your relationship store. Make the space for this to happen. Below is a suggested format for Family Meetings. Use this to get started. Over time you can tweak it to make it your own. Here's what to do:

Stick to the Ground Rules
Family Meetings aren't designed to be gripe sessions. Yes, sometimes they can feel like that. That's because you have to get the problems on the table before you can figure out a solution.

Using the suggested Ground Rules (see Chapters Four and Five for the basic Ground Rules) will help you. When you have a discussion, and no matter how long you have been together, use the basic parameters.

Next, add these:

- **You are learning how to live with each other.** It doesn't matter if this is your First Five-Year Marriage or your tenth. Always keep in mind that you are learning how to live together – *in **this** marriage* (and that will be different from previous marriages). As you learn more about each other, including each other's strengths and limitations, peculiarities, quirks, and eccentricities, you'll find things you like more about your partner. At the same time, some of the things that you once thought were oh-so-cute or funny, might now be driving you crazy; those things are neither cute nor funny now.

That's really normal. It's part of learning how to live with each other.

It's also part of learning to live with change. People change. You will *both* change over five years. When you do, some behaviors will come and others will go.

It's all part of living together, and you will continue to learn how to live together through changes you both make. As long as the changes aren't one of your deal-breakers, you can make agreements and adjust.

Marriage is the ultimate learning experience!

- **Your relationship is your safe space.** Think of your Family Meeting like you're in Vegas: What happens in Family Meetings *stays* in Family Meetings. It should be your safe space. If you can't comfortably share your problems and concerns with your partner, who *can* you share them with? If one of you does (or doesn't do) something and you feel insecure with the relationship, you need to talk about it. And you agree not to bring it up outside of the Family Meeting – like during an argument – or with others.
  - o This does not apply in the case of abuse or abusive behavior.

- **You are entitled to have boundaries, and they need to be respected.** Boundaries matter in any relationship, even in marriage. But I think they are *especially* important in your Five-Year Marriage. Be clear about your boundaries. See Chapter Five for more on this subject.

Keep using the Ground Rules. As you do, you will get more and more comfortable with them over time. Next, always…

Turn the Communication Key
I once asked a marriage counselor what are the three most important skills a couple needs to have a successful marriage. He laughed. "You

know that old real estate thing about location, location, location? Well, in marriage it's communication, communication, communication."

How can you get better at living together, or feel safe, or have personal boundaries that are respected if you don't have strong communication? How can you ever solve problems?

Communication is the cornerstone of your relationship. The marriage counselors know it, marriage mediators know it, even the fifty-years-married Sylvia (whom you met in Chapter Four) knows it. Now, *you have to know it.*

If you talk to therapists and coaches, you'll find out that they see too many people who don't understand what actual communication is. Specifically, people don't seem to understand that communication is a two-way street. When you're living the Five-Year Marriage, you have to be clear that both of you have a voice in the relationship. Also, you both have the responsibility of using that voice to articulate your feelings, your needs, and what's important to you.

In addition to being able to tell your spouse what you need and developing the know-how for solving problems together in a constructive manner, you show respect for each other through your interpersonal communication skills. When those things are lacking or slacking, you're on dangerous ground. Here's a list of some "communication worms" that will eat away at those loving feelings and rot your partnership:

- **One-way talk.** Have you ever talked to your partner when s/he is watching something on television or playing a game? Your partner's attention is on what s/he is doing. S/he responds to you with an "uh-huh" or a "yes, dear" kind of comment. You think s/he is listening and responding, but s/he really isn't. You might be talking but the other person is engaging in meaningless lip service. If that happens *sometimes*, but not often, it could be annoying but not a problem.

  However, when it's a *pattern* of behavior, you run the risk of saying something that's really important, thinking you have agreement, and taking an action with which your partner may not agree. That opens a space for an argument and/or a serious problem.

If you notice that's happening regularly, bring it up at a Family Meeting. Discuss why it's happening. "You know I can't focus while I'm watching the game," may not be a good reason, but it's honest. It's something you can work with to find a solution.

- **Talking "at" your partner.** There is a difference between talking "with" and talking "at" your partner. Talking "with" means that you are in rapport with the other person. You notice the other person's reaction and you respond accordingly.

  Talking "at" your partner means that you're talking but not noticing your partner's reaction. Your partner could be responding with a hurt look, or be surprised or angered by what you are saying. Yet you don't even see the reaction because you're busy expounding on some subject. It's like when people say, "I didn't think s/he would ever stop talking. I couldn't get a word in edgewise. I tried, but s/he didn't even notice. I think s/he just loves the sound of his/her own voice."

- **Non-verbal disrespect.** Communication isn't just the words you say. Communication is also the tone you use when you say it. Many times the tone of your voice frames what you are saying. More arguments have started over *how* something was said than *what* was said. Simple words like "Yes, dear" can be said with tones of love, agreement, resignation, or sarcasm. In turn, the way those words are received can be with openness, understanding, rejection, or anger.

  Sometimes it's not just words or tone of voice, but also body language. If you're talking and your partner rolls his/her eyes, that's a communication problem. Or, if your partner gives you the "cocktail stare" – s/he is looking at you but s/he is clearly thinking about something else – that's a communication problem. Behaviors like eye rolling and cocktail stares are bad manners with anyone and especially bad manners with your spouse and partner. They'll shut down a debate fast!

- **Corrosive Communication**. You *must* have Zero Tolerance for these:
    - **Dishonesty:** overt lying or omission (not telling the whole truth)

    - **Bullying:** silent treatment, temper tantrums, passive-aggressive behavior, etc.

    - **Condescension:** a tone of voice or specific words that make you feel inferior or less than others

    - **Defensiveness:** agitation and a "what do you mean I do [x]...no I don't" attitude

    - **Irrational Anger**: unreasonable or out of control behavior that shuts down the conversation immediately (and may do more and worse)

    - **Personal Insults:** Single words or whole phrases about appearance or behavior designed to hurt feelings and damage closeness
        - "You look like an old mop." (from *Bridesmaids*)
        - "I'll explain and I'll use small words so that you'll be sure to understand, you warthog-faced buffoon." (from *Princess Bride*)

    - **Distort and Distract**: Distorting your (valid) complaint or critiquing it into something ludicrous, making you seem ridiculous to say anything. It could be something like, "Sure, I pick my teeth, each and every one of them, all day long. *It's all I do.* And I'm the *only person in the world* who does it. I should be flogged in the public square."
        - A lot of people use this practice regularly because, by the time your partner is finished

distorting what you said, your point sounds ridiculous, you're belittled, and your whole conversation is distracted. This is a very manipulative practice. Unfortunately, it's commonplace in all kinds of conversations. If you or your partner is doing it, you need to come up with an agreement to stop.

○ **Emotional Disengagement:** Lack of willingness to invest your time and energy in the relationship. Here's how one woman describes this type of corrosive communication: "We live separate lives except for holidays with the kids, business events, and some social gatherings. Other than that, he goes his way and I go mine." When you have emotional disengagement, you and your partner talk to each other but it's about the "necessaries" like the kids, house, and bills (much more business than personal).

The most effective way to get better at communication is by making a joint decision to do it together. If you need guidance, you can read a book (like the *Five-Year Marriage*), take a class, or watch a video. *See the RESOURCES section of this book for some suggestions.*

Then **Practice-Practice-Practice** what you learn. At first, it'll be trial and error. It could seem like it's slow going. Yet, if you are willing to work on it, you will get better at it. Gradually, you'll start noticing that the effort pays off.

Good communication results in true intimacy. And, after all, isn't true intimacy what most people *really* want?

Remember Your Purpose
Before you took your vows and committed five years to each other, you shared what was good about being a couple and why you were choosing to be together. You figured out your purpose (see Chapter Four). When partners forget the "what" and the "why," one or both spouses end up in limbo.

So, when you have a Family Meeting, remind each other, including:

- **You are partners *on purpose*.** That means you're on each other's side and you've got each other's back. If that's not happening, or if one of you isn't feeling it, you need to talk about it.

- **Your purpose has meaning.** It's what you talked about in Chapter Four. You developed your own couple's "shared vision." Those thoughts and ideas will work best if you put them into a sentence or a paragraph that makes you both feel good. Or, boil your purpose into a single word, a phrase or even a song title. The 1987 song "Nothing's Gonna Stop Us Now" by Jefferson Airplane was one that Joseph and I used for a few marriages.

Keep your purpose visible to the two of you but private. Make sure your purpose statement is in a place where you can see it (maybe on a piece of paper in your wallet or as a picture hanging in your bathroom, bedroom or closet). Then talk about it at Family Meetings, including how you think you're doing in living up to that purpose.

When you discuss your purpose, make it a pleasant experience. Have a nice dinner together without kids, TV – in other words, no distractions. It's just the two of you talking about what you agreed is important and meaningful to the two of you. It's remembering who you were at the beginning and talking about how you are progressing through that purpose.

Remember to "high five" or toast yourselves for doing a good job.

Make Magic with Habits
Scientific research says that your brain is always searching for ways to save effort. That's why you have a morning routine that you do without thinking. It's why you drive to work on the same route and fix your coffee the same way. It's a habit. No effort. You do it automatically.

There's something to be said about the power of habits in your Five-Year Marriage too. Much of your relationship will run itself by habits that group themselves into patterns of behavior. Your behaviors will greatly color your relationship.

Developing good couple-habits will save you both time and effort, and most likely, disagreements. They will also positively impact the bonds between you and your spouse.

The opposite is also true.

For example, remember how polite you two were when you were first dating? You said "please," "thank you," and "excuse me." You called each other if you were going to be late. You apologized when you said something rude, or offensive, or made a mistake.

Do you still do that with each other?

Falling out of the good and loving behaviors you once had with each other is a recipe for disaster. At first it doesn't seem so bad. After all, you *do* live together. *How polite do you have to be?* But then s/he notices that you're more polite to your co-worker, a friend, and even the server at your favorite restaurant. It hurts in the short term but, in the long run, it crushes what you have together.

While it's a huge temptation to let some of your dating courtesies go by the wayside, avoid doing it. Instead, make courtesy habits part of your Five-Year Marriage.

Think about these and ask yourself (and each other):

- Have you gotten out of the habit of showing each other the respect of simple courtesies?
    - Do you wish your spouse "Good Morning" when you get up and also greet him/her when s/he comes home?
    - Do you say "excuse me" when you belch or fart?
    - Do you remember to say "please" when you ask your spouse for something?
    - Do you remember to say "thank you" when s/he does what you ask or does something nice for you?

- o Have you stopped saying "God bless you" when s/he sneezes?

- Do you interrupt your spouse when s/he is talking?

- Have you started talking over your spouse when you are with others? That is, when your spouse is telling a story, do you jump in and take over? Or do you interrupt so many times that it ruins the point or the fun of the story?

- Do you "muzzle" your spouse's conversation? That is, is there a laundry list of topics s/he doesn't want you to talk about with others? "Don't tell anyone about my/your family," or "don't tell anyone I am/you are a [political party].

For one woman, muzzling started innocently enough when she complained of her dissatisfaction with her wedding photos. To her surprise, her spouse said he didn't want her sharing her wedding picture displeasure with anyone. She thought his request was too silly to argue with, so she went along.

However, it didn't stop there. Next it was not to joke about silly stuff that happened between them. Then it was something else…and another and another.

The list grew. Eventually she realized her speech was curtailed and, when she wanted to express her honest opinions, she relied on the confidence of only close friends and private conversations.

NOTE: muzzling is different from a *joint decision* to keep certain things private. Many people don't want to discuss finances or they want to wait until the fourth month of pregnancy to tell people. Also, there are the time-honored taboos of politics and religion and you both know, with certain people, those topics will start an argument. So you *both* decide it's better to stay away from those hot button issues when with them. That's a joint decision, not one forced on a single partner (a muzzle).

All of the above revolve around courtesy habits; they count. Contrary to popular practice, politeness doesn't stop after you marry. Small courtesies go a very long way in smoothing over rough spots.

Other habits count too. What other agreements can you have and what habits and behaviors support your agreements?

What if you have an agreement around money, such as saving a certain amount of money each month? What habit(s) will serve that agreement? If you have a goal around saving money to buy a new house, choose an amount (like your future mortgage payment) and have that amount automatically deducted from your paycheck each week. That's just one good money-saving habit that supports your joint agreement to save money. There are others. Find what works for you and get it in place so that it's automatic. When it's a habit, you won't even have to think about it. And you'll get to your goal.

What if you have conflicting habits and goals?

Say you agree to have a weekly date night. So, each week the two of you meet at your favorite bar for Happy Hour and enjoy a couple drinks and appetizer specials. Afterward, you go to dinner together. That's a good date night habit. It can also be an *expensive* habit. It may not be a problem *unless* it keeps you from saving money for that new house.

What do you do?

Look to your joint goals. You want to have a weekly date night. However, if you're saving money to buy a house, and the money you use for your Friday night date is delaying that goal, make a change of habit.

Instead of going out to dinner after drinks and appetizers, take in a movie at home, or walk around your town together, or snuggle up in your car and listen to your favorite music. Or, if you enjoy going out to dinner, choose to make three of those weekly date nights a home-based happy hour followed by, say, a pizza and a DVD. Then, on the fourth week of the month, do the whole drinks and dinner thing.

However you do it, you *can* find a conflict-free way to accommodate both your goals.

What about your other living together habits? Do they support your Five-Year Marriage agreements, or sabotage them?

Do you have an agreement to keep the house straightened up...but you aren't? As you live your Five-Year Marriage, are you both responsible for keeping the bathroom clean? Do one or both of you have a habit not cleaning up after yourself at the sink, toilet, or in the shower? Maybe you habitually leave shoes or clothes around or never turn off the lights.

What if one of you is missing the neatness gene and your stuff is all over? Maybe both of you are like that.

Every one of those issues can be resolved with a new habit...and then you won't have to think about or deal with neatness again, or at least not as often.

What kind of habits can you put into place to help? Take them one step at a time, such as, making a new habit called "No Clothes on the Floor" or "We Each Hang Up All Our Clothes Before We Go to Bed."

Shortly before Joseph and I got married the first time, Marie, the friend of a friend, told me her spouse, Ralph, had a habit of not cleaning the sink after he shaved. In the beginning Marie didn't say anything. But, by year two, she got really tired seeing a sink full of whiskers. It aggravated her to have to clean the sink before she brushed her teeth.

Marie asked Ralph – many times – to clean up after himself. He said he would. She thought they had an agreement. But Marie quickly found out it was just lip service.

By year three, Marie was pregnant and the sight of the dirty bathroom sink each morning made her nauseous. She resented Ralph's empty promise and felt he didn't care about her.

Pregnancy exacerbated Marie's negative feelings toward Ralph. Every morning that whisker-filled sink reinforced her belief that Ralph didn't even care enough about Marie to take fifteen seconds to rinse the sink. Not living up to his agreements made Marie feel disrespected.

A fire of bitterness started inside Marie. Each dirty sink fanned the flames of Marie's fiery "I'm not important to you" narrative. When other things happened, big or small, they were just one more log on the raging fire of Marie's resentment.

Of course, a dirty sink wasn't the final straw that ended the marriage. However, it was one of the many little things that added up and contributed to its demise.

By the way, in case you didn't know…

There is *no* toilet paper fairy who changes the roll, *no* ice cube fairy who fills the tray when it's empty and, when the kids you're watching all afternoon are your own, you aren't "babysitting" them. Make it a habit that whoever gets the next to the last ice cube refills the whole tray. And whoever gets close to the end of the toilet paper either replaces the roll or gets the next refill ready.

The reason those seemingly minor offenses or infringements make such a big deal isn't because one partner *can't* change the toilet paper or fill the ice cube tray or do the dishes. It's because leaving those small things undone can make one partner feel like s/he isn't respected in the relationship.

Little slights add up – and they can easily be avoided through the "magic power" of habits.

Make the Most of Your Family Meetings
During your Five-Year Marriage, human nature being what it is, you are both likely to slip up on your agreements. Also, you are almost destined to do some things that make your partner feel like you don't care. You probably won't mean to do it. Still, if s/he feels you aren't living up to the agreements you made together, that's bad. What do you do? Depending on what it is, you can discuss it during your Family

Meeting and clear the air. Or you can create a habit that helps both of you "mind the store" better.

Here's how to best utilize your Family Meetings:

1. **Decide on the frequency.** This could vary depending on what's going on. Weekly meetings are good at the very beginning. When things are moving easily for the two of you (and you *both* feel that way), monthly meetings work fine. Sometimes you'll need to go back to weekly meetings. Other times you can have quarterly meetings. However, if you notice that too much "stuff" builds up over three months, choose to go back to monthly, biweekly, or weekly meetings. NOTE: when there's a lot going on around or between you, and you feel like you're on different planets, have weekly meetings until things settle down.

   I know it's sometimes inconvenient to have a Family Meeting. However, as I said earlier: you will either *find* time for your relationship or *make* time for your divorce.

2. **Set it up.** Decide on a time and date commitment. Write it on your personal calendar *and* the house calendar. Text each other a reminder in advance.

3. **Choose the place.** As mentioned in the *Ground Rules for Beginners* in Chapter Four, I'm partial to book stores and coffee shops. I also like visiting libraries, museums, and even my local botanical garden (during the off-season). You can find a couple of go-to places where you both feel comfortable and where you have quiet and space.

4. **Keep Family Meetings relatively short** (about 60-90 minutes). If you don't get everything done in the agreed upon time, stop. But before you leave the table, set up another meeting soon, maybe within the week (instead of waiting a month).

NOTE: Sometimes Joseph and I get to the end of our specified time, but we're really getting somewhere. We usually opt to stay and get it done, unless we're really bleary-eyed or hungry and on the verge of getting cranky.

5. **Stick to your favorite set-up**. Since we are all such creatures of habit, when you are in your meeting, it's a good idea to set up a standard way you want to use your meetings. Make that your pattern for the Family Meeting. When you both know the habitual format for Family Meetings, you will both be mentally prepared. And, since you know what you're going to do in the Family Meeting, you will relax – and will get more done.

Here's a suggested format for having substantive Family Meetings:
- Quickly go over the Ground Rules – just as a reminder.
- Review your shared values and your purpose.
- Look at what's working and what's not (see more below).
- When you see what's not working, determine the root cause of a problem, e.g. lack of communication or getting away from good habits.
- Discuss how to resolve the problem.
- Make a commitment to the resolution.

What's Working - What Are We Doing Right?

When you are learning to live together in this Five-Year Marriage, and when you have an argument, sometimes it can seem like all you both have are complaints. Most likely that's not true, but perception can feel like reality.

To keep that from happening, once you get your Family Meetings in place and have planned something worthwhile to discuss, start off on a high note. This is a good time to share with each other what's working well. Describe what you appreciate about your partner and your plans. You can say something like:

- "We said we were going to save $XXX, and we did it. Good for us!"
- "I hated renovating that room, but doing it saved us so much money. And now it's done and it looks great. Yayyy!"
- "I don't know how we got through [X] but we did."
- "I know we're not there yet, but I can see progress."
- "I know you're not there yet, but I can tell you're making an effort."

When you finish, give yourselves a high five or a fist bump or do something upbeat that recognizes your improvement.

The Family Meeting is also the perfect opportunity to praise your partner for something s/he did *just for you*. You did that when you were dating, didn't you? It generated warm feelings that contributed to why you fell in love, *right*?

One of the biggest love traps you want to avoid is having a partnership where all the positive feedback comes from people outside the relationship. If all the "good stuff" comes from outside, for example from friends and co-workers, *what's to keep your partner with you*?

So pay attention to the good behaviors of your partner and say things like:

- "Nice job!"
- "That made me feel good when you complimented me in front of my friends/your parents."
- "I really appreciated when you stopped at the store and picked up [my laundry] for me. It saved me a trip and I got more done here."
- "I notice you're really trying to [be less critical, put the toilet seat down, make a greater effort to be on time, etc.] Thank you!"
- "Thanks for being so nice to my boss. You made me feel proud that we're together."

We all love a pat on the back. There's nothing wrong with giving each other – and your relationship – a decent round of applause. It generates good feelings and a sense of accomplishment.

All in all, Family Meetings are the optimal occasion to recognize what you are both doing right, as individuals and as couples.

NOTE: Don't be stingy and save positive feedback just for Family Meetings. It's a good idea to make a daily habit of telling your spouse what's good about them and your relationship.

What's not working and how can we improve?

When you two discuss the "what's working" part first, you feel confident that some things are going in the right direction. That makes the "not working" part a little less threatening and a little easier to discuss.

Sometimes the things that get under your partner's skin the most are ones that seem totally unimportant to you. But they aren't unimportant, at least not to your partner. Often they have to do with mundane, everyday occurrences like phone habits, food shopping, unexpected bills, in-laws, car troubles, letting go of bad habits, and boring and seemingly thankless tasks. It's surprising how often couples have a united front during a major challenge but things unravel over day-to-day issues. So, to help you sort them out, here are some common ones:

- **Finances.** What arguments and problems are you having about money? Is one partner spending money in a way that's not in keeping with your budget or agreement? Are both of you? How can you make it better?

- **Third wheels.** Is there an extra person in your marriage, like a mother-in-law, child from a previous marriage, a kid sister, or a best friend?

  Only two of you can be living your Five-Year Marriage. You and your spouse are the partners. Everyone else's interference, opinion, and input should be moot. That doesn't mean you don't have a relationship with others. It means you keep relationships with family and friends in perspective and in balance.

- **Facetime**. Are you both so busy with work, house stuff, and children that you aren't seeing each other alone except at bedtime? Are you letting your life be only about the business of your marriage and not the fun of it?

  What if one of you gets a promotion resulting in too frequent travel and it's keeping you apart more than you want? That's a big shift from your Five-Year Marriage agreement.

  You MUST talk about the what (What's in it for us?), the why (Why is this change good for us?), and the how (If we think this can be a long-term benefit, how can we make it work?).

  Then, ask each other:
  o   When can we carve out a chunk of focused time to be together?
  o   How often can we have a date night?
  o   What are our favorite things and what do we enjoy doing when we're together?
  o   How can we integrate those into our weekly activities?

- **Sex**. One of you wants sex more than the other - or not at all. You don't know if you are sexually compatible anymore…and maybe you never were. So talk about it. There are many books, movies, and "spice shops" that can help you get things going. If they don't work, and talking about it doesn't resolve anything, consider seeing a marriage counselor.

- **Children**. One of you wants a child (or another child) now and the other doesn't. There isn't an easy way through this one. However, if you're the one who wants to change your agreement about children, you have to make the case for doing that: financially, physically, emotionally, and logistically.

Maybe you have all the children you want. Perhaps the disagreement isn't over expanding your family but over discipline, helicopter parenting, or spoiling. Maybe your disagreements are more specific, such as splitting responsibilities or taking care of the children – feeding them, doing homework, disciplining them, and all the other good stuff that goes with parenting? If you decided to co-parent, *are you*? If not, what can you do to make that be different?

Maybe the topic isn't about children in *your* Five-Year Marriage, but about issues around children from previous relationships. Again, any time you are making decisions about children, remember, *they didn't ask to be born*. You *chose* to bring them into the world.

Children difficulties are tender ones. Sometimes a professional mediator can be helpful. Mediation isn't free. However, the cost of a marriage mediator isn't as expensive as an attorney or going to court with an ex. To find a marriage mediator, check the links in *RESOURCES*.

- **Technology**. Past generations didn't have to deal with this, and maybe they had an advantage. Technology has become a problem in many relationships. Texting, surfing, non-stop phone checking, and seeing who is connecting with you on Facebook, Instagram, or Twitter is not as important as giving your partner your whole attention when the two of you are together. Selfish technology behaviors are seriously impacting emotional intimacy between partners.

How important is it to check a text message when you and your spouse are having a conversation or when you are out together? Unless there's something big going on, like a child or parent is sick or you're on call with work (and you're both in agreement that you might get a call), checking your phone or interacting on social media *is not important*. When you are out with your spouse, s/he is the only important person, your only priority.

165

If you did not figure this into your Five-Year Marriage agreement yet, do it now. Chances are it wasn't a problem then. If it is now, figure out a fair and balanced way, that you *both* can agree on, for integrating phones and social media into your life.

- **Smothering or soloing.** Are you giving each other enough privacy and alone time? Or is it too much time?

Many women complain that they can't even have privacy in the bathroom. Your uninterrupted shower time might be your best time to focus your day. Maybe it's just that you feel you have no space to be alone; you hate that you can't even pee alone. That's a problem. And it's not just because of the kids.

What kind of alone time do you need? Twenty minutes to meditate? A half hour of bathroom time in the morning? What do you need? And how can you and your partner work it out?

Or you aren't feeling smothered; instead you feel the opposite. Maybe you are alone too much. S/he is busy with work, kids, sports, television, the internet, or something else and too busy to be alone with you.

Maybe one of you is obsessed with sports; you need to talk about it. Sports aren't a bona fide addiction, but if you are watching games all day Saturday and Sunday and several nights a week, what is your partner doing? If s/he isn't with you *and enjoying the same activity*, you may have a problem that you need to work out.

Maybe it's not sports. Maybe it's binge-watching television shows. Or getting lost in a hobby, like jewelry-making or golf. Time-wise, all those activities amount to the same thing as sports.

Suggestion: Pick one day that's a "binge day" for whatever leisure activity you are obsessed with. It can be one day a week or one day a month. When you make a binge-day agreement, stick to it. Marriage is a team sport and you and your partner need to be on the same team and playing on the same field.

NOTE: If one of you needs and wants more alone time - instead of more time alone with your spouse - that will probably put a serious strain on any marriage. You are in a marriage to have someone to share your time with, someone with whom you can travel through life. Most people don't think it's fun to travel alone.

Living-together-loneliness is one of the bigger complaints in marriage. It's certainly more common than having too much together time.

If it's happening with you, it's a "red flag" that you need to address before starting another Five-Year Marriage.

- **Speech ticks.** Constant interrupting constitutes a major problem in many relationships. So is rambling or consistently distracted conversation. Any of those can demoralize your relationship. If that's a problem in your marriage, you need to talk about it, specifically why it happens and what you can do about it. For example, if it's interrupting, what's going on that allows the offending partner thinks it's OK to interrupt?

Interrupting is a behavior that's very easy to notice. But what if it's rambling, cursing, or some other interpersonal communication gaffe?

Speech ticks might be ignored when you're dating. But when you're trying to work something out, solve a problem, and come to a new agreement, they can be a serious distraction and even a conversation killer.

If one (or both) of you has a speech tick, find a respectful solution.

- **Overcare.** Overcare means being so overly caring for everyone else that you don't have any time for yourself. Overcare comes from a lack of balance between self-care and caring. Overcare eventually leads to burnout.

When living the Five-Year Marriage, if one partner is doing more than his/her share, go back to your original agreement. Are you each living up to your agreements? If not, *how* not? What can you do about it?

It's good to pay attention to overcare (and undercare), so you can bring it up during a Family Meeting. Also, you need to notice so you can rethink your agreement for your next Five-Year Marriage.

- **Addiction.** What if one of your careers becomes more demanding and the stress causes one partner to drink too much or take drugs? What if one partner is getting on porn sites regularly? Maybe you aren't sure it's reached the point of addiction yet, but you need to talk about it – *now*.

If something isn't working...

It doesn't matter if this is your first marriage or your fifth one. Over the course of five years, things happen that change you. When you change, your relationship changes, and your partnership can shift. You aren't tied indefinitely to the same old same old, and that's one of the beauties of the Five-Year Marriage.

Some of the agreements you made in Marriage#1 are likely to need adjustment or replacement in Marriage#2. However, you can only consider new agreements if you're paying attention (minding the store) and communicating with each other with love. When all you know is that something is not the same (that is, different from what you agreed to) and you don't feel good about it, that's a problem. But that problem cannot be solved *unless* you:

- Are paying attention to what's working and what's not.

- Can articulate your positive and negative thoughts and feelings – that is, why something is a problem for you.
- Come to the Family Meeting with a few suggestions for staying in tune with each other. It's wise for each of you to have a couple of ideas that you can toss around, adjust, etc. What will make it better for you?
- Can both *honestly* agree on the solution.

What happens at the end of five years?

That's up to you.

As mentioned earlier, Joseph and I typically anticipate the end of our marriage in year four, usually a few months in advance of the end-date. Before we make the decision to have another marriage, we look at how our Five-Year Marriage is winding down. We have more heart-to-hearts to discuss what we would do if we stayed together another five years. We go back to the *Five-Year Marriage Basics: The Beginnings* and review our *Nitty Gritty* essentials, the nuts and bolts of our life for this Five-Year Marriage.

Doing that together is healthy. It makes room for any changes of feelings. It also acknowledges the changes both around us and between us.

Through several Five-Year Marriages, this process seems to be the same. My experience is that it starts out as fun, even sweet. It's heartwarming and gratifying to remember the good times. It's life-affirming to realize what you've accomplished and overcome together. When you start looking ahead, the conversations start shifting between challenging and scary.

Some Five-Year Marriages don't always have an upside. During any given Five-Year Marriage you could experience an illness, a downturn, or a tragedy. It's important to make that a part of your discussion.

So, when *your* Five-Year Marriage is almost over, how do you take your next step?

FIRST, go back to the *Five-Year Marriage Basics: The Beginnings* and *The Nitty Gritty* chapters. Review and refresh your thoughts about marriage, values, purpose, and goals. Keep those things in mind and use them to help frame your contract for the next five years.

Also, talk about your now-ending marriage. Here are a few questions to ask each other. They'll get you on a good track and moving forward:

- What were some of our best moments of the past five years?

- What's changed during the Five-Year Marriage? Did one or both of us change jobs or careers, move to a new home, move as a result of a job change, have children, become caregivers, or have a change of health or physical ability. Or is there something else?

- What energized me in our relationship?

- What drained me?

- How well did we deal with conflicts (or not)?
    - What did I like about how we handled one challenge or another (talk about the specific challenges you faced)?
    - What bothered me most about how we dealt with them?
    - How well did we fight?
    - How do I think we could fight better and handle conflicts more effectively?

- What five times stand out in my mind when I felt most loved by you?

- When did I make you feel special and what did I do that made you feel that way?

- Here's how I can envision the next five years could playing out for us...

- If everything could work out the way I want,
    - I think our biggest challenge would be...

    o Our biggest win would be....

- If we stay together, here's my biggest fear for the next five years...

- If we stay together, here's my biggest wish for the next five years...

Using those questions as your springboard, plan your next five years. Don't forget to WRITE IT DOWN. You can make a lot of promises but unless they're written down, you'll forget them.

THEN WHAT?

That will depend on (1) if you decide to get married again, (2) how much of a celebration you want to have and (3) what your finances look like.

If you decide *not* to have another Five-Year Marriage...

- Figure out your new living arrangements
- Decide what to do about the children (you should already have an agreement about this that will guide you)
- See an attorney
- Tell the children **together**

If you are choosing to stay together, and you have already done the work of putting your Five-Year Marriage agreement together, here are some celebration suggestions:

- Have another wedding and invite only the people you really want
- Have a ceremony for just you and your children at your favorite family-friendly vacation spot
- Have a small, private ceremony followed by a party at your house
- Combine a destination wedding with your vacation

Whatever you do, *make it something special*. You don't know what the next five years will bring. No time is promised to anyone.

Yet, you know what you've been through together and you're choosing to face the world and life together again…at least for another five years.

That's a big deal. Make sure to honor your decision by celebrating your new union.

During one Five-Year Marriage, whatever we planned in advance of our wedding got absorbed by the caregiving we gave to our mothers. And it started on the day of our wedding. It was September 2008 and the world's finances were in turmoil. We expected to have a blessing at the Valley Forge Chapel, but the minister temporarily suspended services for personal reasons (read more about this in Chapter One).

That probably worked out because, as the primary caregivers for our mothers, Joseph and I spent the morning figuring out what we had to do to protect our mothers' finances. Later that day we went to the chapel and had a private service.

Between that marriage and the next one in 2013, we used whatever time would have gone to our own goals to make our mothers lives easier or more comfortable in their final years. They both had needs, and those needs usually had to be addressed at the same time. So that's what we did. When they died, we had to settle their estates, small though they were. By the time everything was complete, it was the end of our marriage.

As we looked back on that Five-Year Marriage, we realized that our relationship had become somewhat frozen in time. Though it was something of a milestone (25 years in traditional years), we were, in terms of purpose and goals, at about the same place we were in 2008. Yet time had moved on around us. Joseph and I had to face the fact that we were twenty-five years older than our first wedding day. We no longer had "forever" in front of us.

Because we had more to think about and discuss, Joseph and I started our contracting conversations in February 2013. They weren't easy.

We started with the usual "Where do we want to go in the next five years?" talk. However, after twenty-five years, we faced the realization that we were no longer in the "start-up" phase of our lives. We needed to evaluate our finances and think about the future in a different way. It wasn't comfortable and took a long time.

That year it took us until mid-September to finally get our plans in order. We decided to marry again. That year we were married at the Tyler Arboretum (described in Chapter One).

Chapter Six: Joseph's Take

If Annmarie and I didn't *live* our Five-Year Marriage, this book probably wouldn't have been possible. It was in our Family Meetings (especially the big one that ended the last marriage and began this Five-Year Marriage), that Annmarie and I discussed making this book happen. We both agreed that writing this book was a top priority. It took a long time because we both work full-time and have pretty busy lives.

In the months before this book was finished, many of our Family Meetings were either about making some changes in our responsibilities so the book could get finished or going over chapters and making sure we were being honest and straight about what we've done.

The Family Meetings gave us direction together. I don't like to be blindsided, so for me, the Family Meetings help me know where we're going next. They also help me to know what to do so I don't just focus on my own things.

Living the Five-Year Marriage isn't easy. At the same time, I don't think I'd want it any other way.

Chapter Seven
What About the Children?

Children Learn What They Live
Dorothy Law Nolte, Lifelong Educator

"Do you have children?"

That's the first question people almost always ask when they hear about the Five-Year Marriage. When I tell them I *don't* have any children, the next question is usually, "What happens to the kids in a Five-Year Marriage?"

I think it's a curiously odd question. I wonder why someone would think to ask *that* question *only* about the Five-Year Marriage.

Considering the divorce rate, why doesn't everyone have that *same* concern about children in a *traditional* marriage? After all, there *is* an almost 50% divorce rate for first marriages. It's even higher for second and third marriages. Wouldn't it be just as logical to ask this of engaged couples, traditionally married newlyweds and living-together couples: *"What's going to happen to your children if you break up?"* Wow! Wouldn't couples be horrified to be asked that question?

Yes, it's a logical question, but it doesn't happen. Typically, most people stay out of other people's traditional marriages. Think about it. Probably *at least* one couple in your circle of friends has a relationship that is destined for divorce (yes, you know who they are, don't you?). Do you ever ask *that* couple how the children are handling their obvious incompatibility? *No, you don't.* You mind your own business. Yet many children live in friction-filled households for years – maybe the entire time they are growing up. If you suspect a problem, you may worry about them, even pray for them. *But you don't interfere.*

Still, everyone knows that the prelude to divorce is almost always years in the making. What couple wakes up one morning and decides they

175

don't want to be married anymore? They don't. Even in the case of addiction, abuse, and infidelity, the decision is almost never sudden.

In the months or years before a couple decides to divorce, many couples think they hide the tension between them from their children. They don't.

If the couple has children, they *are* affected. Children absorb the negativity in the house. They hear the arguments. They see the looks of disdain or hurt or anger. Any fear they have over their parents splitting up begins long before the separation.

If that's the case, how often does *anyone* express concern to a quarrelling and seemingly discordant couple about the physical, mental, emotional, and spiritual well-being of their children? Does *anyone* do that?

Okay, yes, there *are* exceptions. Sometimes a grandparent or a good friend will see a divorce in the making and voice a concern for the children. Though it doesn't happen too often, when it does, the concern *might* be acknowledged. If my Mom had said something to me, I *might* have listened because I knew she was asking out of concern. I would also have told her it was alright and not to worry. I *might* make an exception for my mother, and *maybe* for my father. But I probably wouldn't have appreciated it from anyone else.

Yet, most of the time, when a family member or friend expresses concern, one or both of the feuding couple tells the concerned person to butt out. It's none of their business.

Even *during* a divorce, there's a hesitance on the part of "outsiders" to get involved. Maybe your parent or a sibling might contribute with help or money, but usually only if you ask for the assistance.

So it's a mystery to me why so many people express a concern that the children of a Five-Year Marriage would automatically be in a worse or less stable situation. *But they do.* Not only do people ask the question, they even offer an opinion – usually a negative one. Like Janet.

Janet and I were having lunch following an interview I did with her for a Victorious Woman article. It was close to a time when Joseph and I were getting married, so I shared our Five-Year Marriage concept with her. It took almost no time for Janet to demand, "Do you have children?"

"No," I answered.

"Well," she started and then practically spit out the next words. "That's really unfair to the children. *You* don't have children so *you* don't know how *that* kind of relationship [a Five-Year Marriage] would affect them. It's *really* unfair."

At first I was a bit taken aback by the vehemence with which Janet spoke. I tried not to feel attacked. Instead I asked questions because I really wanted to understand where she was coming from, what was behind her words.

Yes, it's true I don't have children. However, what Janet didn't know is that my life wasn't then and isn't now devoid of children. I explained that, for many years, I taught elementary and middle school and also served as a Girl Scout leader. During that time I saw very few divorces at the Catholic schools where I worked. However, though couples stayed together, I saw the effects of many unhappy marriages on the children. Also, my girlfriends (so many good Catholic girls!) had lots of children. I babysat many of those children. I was as close to some of them as I was to their parents. They often revealed home life strife without realizing exactly what they were saying.

Thinking about the parents of those children gave me pause. I thought about the many sad and disturbing things I saw between the parents, including sniping, sarcasm, belittling, and other distancing behaviors. I also witnessed the irresponsibility of one parent or another around money, or childcare, or social life.

When I saw what those behaviors did to the kids, my heart would feel sad for those children.

Describing all that to Janet, I asked her, "How much worse could the Five-Year Marriage be for children?" She had no real response except to say that traditional marriage gave children stability.

Just the same, since I've been asked the "Do you have children?" question a lot, I often looked at the pros and cons. More and more, I saw that the Five-Year Marriage would *not* be worse.

In fact, I can see how much *better* for children the Five-Year Marriage could be.

In a traditional marriage, children always presume their parents will stay together. Then, when the parents split, the children are laden with guilt. It's as though the children feel that they are responsible for the breakup. Many children carry that feeling of guilt their entire lives.

On the other hand, the children in a Five-Year Marriage will always know their parents are together for just five years. They know that maybe they will continue and maybe they won't. They will also know that their parents discussed divorce, including what happens to the children, even before they got married. So, for children, that knowledge might be very freeing.

After all, the children would see their parents having ongoing dialogue about their marriage. Those couples would openly acknowledge problems when they come up (presuming age appropriateness). They would also model how to deal with and solve problems through communication and agreement.

Yes, children might see parents get angry and argue in the process. That's part of life. However, they would also see parents using problem-solving skills and maybe seeking outside help when necessary. Children would, almost by osmosis, learn those same problem-solving skills – positive skills they could later use in their own relationships.

In addition, parents would already have made an agreement about the physical and financial needs of their children (just in case they divorced). As a couple, you and your partner would take care of that aspect while planning your marriage, when you are most emotionally able to be positive and put the best interests of your children first. Knowing that could give many children a sense of security.

Still, Janet's comments stuck with me. So I decided to conduct my own study and analysis.

First I looked at the changing face of marriage. Since popular television is a barometer for societal trends, I started there.

As a society, we have changed the definition of a family. In the 1950s and 1960s, the family was defined by a married husband and wife and their children. Television shows like *Father Knows Best* and *Ozzie and Harriet* epitomized that family model.

By the late 1960s and 1970s, the family started looking different. *The Brady Bunch* showcased the blended family. *One Day at a Time* focused on the challenges of a divorced mother raising her two children. *The Andy Griffith Show*, *Different Strokes* and *Full House* showed that dads could manage children and a household without a mom (though Andy had Aunt Bea, Mr. Drummond had a housekeeper, and Danny Tanner had his friends). However, in the sitcom, *Who's the Boss?* Dad Tony Micelli did it all. He took care of the house, did the shopping, made the meals, and handled the childcare for both his own daughter and the son of his employer, Angela, a divorced high-powered advertising executive.

Shifting mores continued through the end of the twentieth century and into the new millennium. The popular *Modern Family* shows the lifestyles of several different kinds of families, including one with two dads. The very funny *Jane the Virgin* makes us laugh with the complications that occur when the virgin is accidently artificially inseminated and becomes a single mother.

In real life, celebrities like Sandra Bullock, Minnie Driver, and Hoda Kotb have modeled single-by-choice motherhood as a viable lifestyle option. The one-parent-by-choice family is no longer very unusual.

So, unlike previous generations, children of the new millennium are used to seeing all kinds of nontraditional relationships being called families. They see them all as normal.

Next, after checking the cultural influences, I studied the research on children, marriage, and divorce.

Studies about traditional marriage and divorce found that an unhappy marriage ending in divorce has a huge impact on children. Without a doubt, divorce seriously affects children. Research shows that children whose parents divorce suffer academically, have behavioral problems, and are more likely to engage in drug and alcohol abuse. In addition, divorce doesn't end when the children are grown.

Children of divorce experience an assortment of dreads including fear of loss, failure, change, abandonment, and conflict. Often the emotional impact lasts for years, maybe even for life. In fact, the greatest impact of divorce on children often doesn't show up until the child enters into an adult relationship.

In one study, researchers Dr. Judith Wallerstein and Dr. Julia M. Lewis followed children of divorce for twenty-five years. They published their findings in their book, *An Unexpected Legacy of Divorce*. Through their study, Wallerstein and Lewis discovered that those fears show up when the adult children enter a serious relationship. The adult children of divorce are more likely to make poor choices in relationships, give up when facing conflict or may even avoid relationships altogether.

Other studies indicate that children of divorce are more likely to view cohabitation without marriage as a good alternative. That's even in spite of the facts that couples who live together have more breakups and even higher incidences of domestic disputes and domestic violence.

What I probed next was how much the divorce itself created those outcomes. Could it be that, *if children learn what they live*, the home life leading up to the divorce is at least as responsible for all the "bad outcomes" as the divorce itself? That makes sense, *doesn't it*?

180

After all, passing a bad relationship onto children is easy when they see:

- Parents always at odds with each other; children presume that's how all relationships are.
- One parent overcaring (doing all the work) while the other parent withdraws; they think that's normal.
- Dad treating Mom like she's stupid or Mom treating Dad like he's a failure; they mimic that behavior.
- Parents arguing, belittling, controlling, bossing, and more; they expect those behaviors in their own relationships.
- Parents using anger or manipulation to solve problems; kids think that's how it's done.
- Domestic abuse or domestic violence; adult children duplicate those practices in his or her own relationships.

Similarly, you've probably heard a man or woman admit, "I married my mother" or "I married my father." It's a common explanation that someone uses to explain why her or his marriage isn't healthy and/or when it ends in divorce.

Given all that research, I can't see the Five-Year Marriage creating a child-Armageddon. If a couple is working the Five-Year Marriage, and even before children are in the picture, they focus more on partnership than turf wars, agreement instead of argument.

In your life, the addition of a child, or children, is a change; children create seismic shifts in a relationship. Still, if you are seriously working the Five-Year Marriage (see Chapter Six, Behind Closed Doors: Living the Five-Year Marriage), Family Meetings are a regular event. You already have a format for discussion and problem solving. As your child gets older, you may even choose to invite him or her into the Family Meeting as soon as s/he has some sense of understanding. You don't have to do that with every Family Meeting, but for a few each year. When you do, your child can see first-hand how discussion and problem solving work.

Next, after looking at the cultural influence and the research, my probing continued.

I decided to do my own (unscientific) study by gathering anecdotal evidence. I talked to adults who were the children of divorce and a few who were raised predominantly by single mothers. I also talked to adults whose parents stayed together "for the children" and didn't divorce until their children were grown.

I wasn't surprised by what I heard. The experiences of the adult children mirrored the research. However, the conversations were not nearly as cut-and-dried. Some of those conversations became *very* personal and emotional.

During those exchanges, several men and women confessed, "I wish they *would have* divorced," explaining, "All they did was fight." For Beth, school was her safe place. "I loved being at school," she admitted, "because nothing changed. There was continuity and a routine and I felt 'normal' there." Others echoed similar sentiments about school, or a sport, or hanging out at a friend's home.

Clearly, those adults didn't experience a normal healthy relationship between the two most important adults in their lives. More than half of the adult children with whom I spoke admitted:

- Their parents seldom had a wholesome/healthy conversation.
- Arguments were common and often a daily occurrence.
- Anything could start a serious argument, from what was for dinner, to how much money was spent, or what it was spent on.
- There was little communication between parents; when their parents *did* talk without arguing, the exchanges were often biting and terse.
- What they remember most is a household usually filled with either acrimony or tension.

One woman, Karen, admitted that, as a child, adult relationships were confusing. "The only time my parents got along," she explained, "was when we had company. Then you would have thought that my parents were the best of friends. I liked having company because I saw the nicer side of my parents together. I think having company might be the only time I felt a sense of security, or maybe it was relief – like maybe things would be good from now on. But it never lasted."

Another woman, Barbara, said, "My father was a jerk. I thought that's how all men were. I didn't know better. So, though I didn't realize it at the beginning, I ended up marrying a man just like him. My first marriage ended in divorce."

One of the luckier ones was Bethany. She was six years old when her parents got a divorce. Before she graduated high school, her mother married two more times. In between marriages, Bethany says, "my Mom dated *a lot*." So when Bethany married her college sweetheart, Mike, she had hope but a lot of trepidation. Bethany and Mike are still married but, she said, "I don't know how I got lucky. I see my sisters and they seem to be following in my mother's footsteps."

Sadly, that outcome is fairly common. Bethany is the exception. Unless the child-turned-adult identifies, names, and claims unproductive behaviors for themselves, and makes a concerted effort to change those behaviors, they will be repeated.

Alisha, a seemingly well-adjusted twenty-something, told me her parents separated when she was twelve. Describing those first couple years, Alisha lived with her mother and, about those earlier years, said "It was really hard at the beginning."

Then, when Alisha was sixteen, her parents got back together. At first she thought the reconciliation was a good thing, but the happy days didn't last long. She described the next few years living with both parents in just a few words: "I couldn't stand it."

It was so bad, according to Alisha, that she had several heart-to-heart talks with her mother. Describing those discussions to me, Alisha actually had a sense of pride about encouraging her mother to finally start divorce proceedings. She even took some credit for finally bringing the unhappy marriage to an end.

Frank, an only child, told me his parents divorced as soon as he went away to college. Though Frank is pretty smart, emotional intelligence isn't his strong suit. Given Frank's lack of interpersonal and social skills, I can only imagine how solitary his life must have been while growing up. When I asked him how he felt when the divorce happened, he got very defensive. *"I don't care* if they got a divorce," he said, sounding rather irritated. "It's none of my business."

Really? *Of course it was his business.* No child lives through a parents' divorce in a vacuum.

Many parents think they keep their rifts between them and hide the resulting acrimony. They don't.

Even when the parents don't argue in front of the children, the icy energy permeates the house. Every child knows when Mom and Dad are angry with each other, even when it's just a small marital spat. When it's more than that, there's no hiding bitterness, hostility, or antagonism when you're all living in the same house.

Years later, when those children are old enough to have their own relationships, they replicate the behaviors they saw growing up. Even when children don't like what they observed, the behaviors are engrained in their psyche.

That was the challenge for Joseph and me. It was an obstacle I wanted to overcome in our Five-Year Marriage.

I'm *not* a child of divorce. Growing up I knew my parents loved each other. But theirs was a very traditional Italian-style marriage in that my father ruled the roost. Also, as a result of war, my father suffered from what we now call post-traumatic stress syndrome (PTSD). He also had many physical ailments. Then, when I was in my teens, my father became an alcoholic. The effects of that illness overshadowed many of the more positive aspects of my parents' relationship.

In addition to those challenges, there was an additional stress. My oldest brother, who was always getting into trouble for as long as I can remember, created friction between my parents. The fights were usually between my brother and my father (over almost anything, but especially over house rules and curfew). My mother would defend my brother, which would anger my father even more. Then my brother would leave the house. But, as he was walking out the front door, he'd say something exceptionally upsetting to my father. I later started calling it the "grenade move" because it was akin to pulling the pin and throwing a grenade into the living room. When it exploded, usually between my father and mother, the rest of us had to deal with the aftermath.

Interestingly, Joseph's family made my family look normal.

Joseph *is* a child of divorce. As explained in Chapter Two, when Joseph was eighteen months old, his father left the family and got a Mexican divorce; his four children never heard from him again.

Though his mother had a very long-term relationship with another man, Vic, he was no father figure. Rhoda and Vic's relationship was what I would call "strangely dependent." They went out each night and partied heartily.

Yet, through most of their relationship, Rhoda and Vic didn't live together, didn't get too involved in each other's lives (like going to family events), and didn't do anything a regular long-time couple might do. They seemed to use each other for social companionship and sex. In fact, it wasn't until close to the end of Vic's life, when all Rhoda's adult children were gone and living elsewhere, that Vic moved in with her.

Interestingly, the only semblance of a father in Joseph's life was his track coach, Jim, a cantankerous man who pushed Joseph and his brother to excel at sports. His mentoring resulted in many achievements that gave Joseph a small sense of confidence and accomplishment.

Still, as children of divorce and alcoholism, Joseph and his siblings didn't have an easy life. Both of Joseph's sisters married early and hastily...and divorced just as quickly. Joseph's oldest sister married again; she has been married for over thirty years. His other sister is twice married and divorced. Joseph's brother married shortly after graduating college, was married for twenty years, and divorced. After the split, he quickly entered a relationship that lasted eight years. That breakup was quickly followed by another marriage.

Unlike his siblings, Joseph dated during college and throughout his twenties, but none of his relationships resulted in a long-term connection. He was in his early thirties when we met.

Between his upbringing and mine, as children of alcoholics and dysfunction, a successful relationship wasn't a safe bet. In retrospect, I imagine, when I first suggested the Five-Year Marriage, Joseph's family history may have something to do with why he was open to trying something different.

The Five-Year Marriage enabled us to design a fairly equal partnership. It provided both of us with a solid model for better marital and relationship communication.

So, will choosing the Five-Year Marriage be better for your children? Will it be the "unfair" situation that Janet insisted it is?

That will be up to you. It will depend on whether you follow the tenets of the Five-Year Marriage. In fact, if you are honest with your children, you can use your Five-Year Marriage as a teaching tool. Through your Five-Year Marriage, your children will see:

- Marriage isn't perfect and it isn't a blissful fairy tale.
- Parents who aren't perfect but who strive for fairness between them.
- Five-Year Marriage commitments make sense.
- A couple who make their relationship a priority.
- There is a purpose and a benefit to working toward a common goal.
- Problems have solutions and can be worked out amicably.
- Solutions don't happen by magic.
- Communication is important.
- Marriage takes a lot of work.
- A Five-Year Marriage breeds love and intimacy.

Of course, just because you have a Five-Year Marriage doesn't mean you aren't going to divorce. *It could happen*. But, if you work the process, you are more likely to have a better shot at creating a healthy environment for yourself and your spouse as well as the children you bring into this world.

Remember that children learn what they live. In your Five-Year Marriage, you are demonstrating healthy behaviors around typical relationship problems. And, since you are committed to your Five-Year Marriage, you are demonstrating that commitment through Family Meetings, healthy arguing, and effective problem solving.

How could those strong relationship skills and positive behaviors be bad for children?

Chapter Seven: Joseph's Take

Because Annmarie and I don't have children, we can't tell any parent how to raise their children. However, *did you know* that by the age of two (yes, two years old!) a child begins to mimic and assume the posture and movement patterns of his or her parents? For example, a child will most likely learn and implement good posture and movement patterns if their parents have good posture and movement patterns. The child is unaware of this learning process. They assume their parent's posture and movement patterns by osmosis.

The same applies to a child's social, physical, emotional, spiritual, and intellectual development. If a child sees his parents sitting down to discuss each of the goals, objectives, and values of their marriage and watches them work to continuously improve their marriage, that's what the child learns is normal.

So, wouldn't it stand to reason that that, as the child grows into adulthood, s/he has a better chance of succeeding in life and having a happy and stable marriage?

Chapter Eight
What People Like You, Ask Me

*A successful marriage requires falling in love many times,
always with the same person.*
Mignon McLaughlin, Journalist and Author

During the twenty-nine years that Joseph and I have been in the unusual arrangement of our Five-Year Marriage, people have had a variety of reactions. As mentioned earlier, when we were younger, few people we shared our idea with took our Five-Year Marriage seriously. Some (the more flippant inquirers) tried figuring out how many marriages (with a variety of people) they could rack up in a lifetime. One person even tried figuring out how to turn the Five-Year Marriage into a divorce-driven money-maker.

More recently, and because Joseph and I are still together, the questions now are usually more serious and thoughtful. Overall, people have a lot of questions about the practicality and viability of having a short-term marriage. Something in their consciousness recognizes a sense and sensibility about a contract marriage. The idea touches off an emotional response they can't explain, but they wanted more of it.

Still, as intrigued by the idea as they might be, they wonder how we have pulled it off. Or maybe more to the point, they wanted to know how they could do the same thing.

Take Cindy, a born-again Christian with whom I served in a professional organization. She *hated* the idea from the first time I shared it with her. Cindy didn't just ask questions; she argued, judged, and quoted the bible. She saw the Five-Year Marriage as a conflict of Christian faith and doctrine. We talked about it whenever I would say something about Joseph or our Five-Year Marriage. After a couple years we both left the organization and lost touch.

My path didn't cross Cindy's for several years. By the time we ran into each other again, her life had taken many twists and turns. At that point, she saw the Five-Year Marriage differently. As a result, her attitude had shifted from judgmental to curious and interested.

Cindy reminds me of so many others who want answers.

In addition to wondering "What about the children?" they are curious about the legality of our relationship, how we handle our finances, and what we think about our futures. And, of course, some skeptics still want to know if Joseph and I take the Five-Year Marriage seriously or if it's a joke.

Clearly inquiring minds want to know. This chapter answers some of the many questions I've been asked in almost thirty years of Five-Year Marriages. If your questions aren't answered here, ask me. I might not have every answer, but if I don't, I can help you find it. Post your questions for me at FiveYearMarriage.com.

1. What is a Five-Year Marriage, that is, how do you define it?

    The Five-Year Marriage is a partnership marriage. As with any partnership, a Five-Year Marriage couple has a contract or agreement. The partnership has an end date. That means that, for the time of the stated partnership, both partners promise to live up to their agreed upon principles, values, and standards as well as pursue shared goals.

    At the end of five years, the partners either create another Five-Year Marriage (with a new contract/agreement) or end the marriage.

2. Why is the marriage for five years? Can't it be one year or ten years?

    Yes, it *could* be any time you want it to be. In Lake Bell's movie, *I Do...Until I Don't*, her character uses a seven-year contract.

    What I didn't realize when I first got the inspiration to create this unconventional marriage was that five years is an ideal timeframe. There are multiple reasons. To begin with, a lot happens to partners, individually and communally, over the course of five years. In five years of living together, you get to see the good, the bad, and the ugly.

By comparison, a one-year or two-year marriage is too short a time. Typically, because life evolves, changes aren't as easy to notice.

Alternatively, a longer marriage defeats the purpose. Over the course of ten years, so much more can and does happen. It's harder to keep track. Facts get hazy, points get lost, life continues to throw more into the mix, and problem solving gets put on the backburner.

Five years allows enough time for the:

- Mental space to think about how your agreement is working out.
- Emotional room to evaluate how you feel.
- Breathing space so you don't feel your decisions are rushed.
- Perspective of performance over time.

In addition, the five-year timeframe gives you wonderful opportunities to study your partnership. If some bad thing happens in year two or three, like maybe you lose a job, cannot conceive a child, or have serious financial problems, you can really find out what your relationship is made of and see the strength of your commitments to each other.

In traditional marriages, many couples, during that midpoint time, decide to go their separate ways. In a five-year marriage, you agree to stay together for the whole time – no divorce, no trial separation – you're in it together through the end of year five. So often that bad thing that could have torn you apart in year three becomes more nuanced by year four. By then you've talked about it, vented your feelings, argued, apologized, and even solved the problem so it doesn't happen again.

Also, if you decide to get married again, you can reach agreement on an entirely new set of matters – ones you didn't even know about in the first marriage. You can agree to be better, and do better, and still be there for each other. That's how a good partnership keeps going, even gets stronger. Five years gives you the time and space to do that.

If you were to marry for just one or two years, you might not notice any change or have time to process your thoughts and feelings from one year to the next. Or you might be enveloped in something, like children, an illness, a career shift, or parental caregiving. When you are deep "in it" you often cannot see the forest for the trees.

One couple who renewed their wedding vows annually did so with some fanfare. To me, it seemed a bit frivolous. I wondered who they were more bent on convincing of their love and devotion, the world or each other? Or, maybe it just simply a great excuse for having a fabulous party. Still, they were into it. Though I might not have agreed, I thought, *if it works for them, who am I to judge*?

Sadly, it *didn't* work for them over the long term. Yet it was fun while it lasted.

Ultimately, what makes the five-year timeframe ideal is because it is both long enough to know what works and what doesn't and short enough to prevent complacence.

3. Is the Five-Year Marriage the same as a pre-nuptial agreement?

No. The Five-Year Marriage is not a prenup. You can include a prenup in your Five-Year Marriage contract but it's not all there is to it. Your Five-Year Marriage isn't focusing on pre-marital assets. It could, but it doesn't have to…because it isn't a prenup.

According to FindLaw.com, "Premarital agreements (also called prenuptial agreements or "prenups") are a common legal step taken before marriage. A prenup establishes the property and financial rights of each spouse in the event of a divorce."

From that perspective, while it's usually for people with a lot of assets, you could include decisions about your finances and property owned previous to the Five-Year Marriage. In addition, you *should* include what happens to your children should you divorce. Logically, that would mean things like how you would share custody, what financial arrangements would be made for them, and what would happen if you divorce and one or both of you gets married again.

The purpose of taking care of the children in advance is so that you are thinking about them while you are both filled with love and before they become emotional footballs in an angry game of divorce.

Does that constitute a pre-nuptial agreement? Not exactly, at least not with the same legal ramifications.

Your Five-Year Marriage focuses on the two of you starting strong with your emotional eyes wide open. It's designed to help each of you become the best kind of marriage partner you can be.

Of course, if you have a lot of financial assets and want to have a prenup, by all means, see an attorney and get one.

Just don't confuse the division of premarital assets, as defined by a prenuptial agreement, with the Five-Year Marriage.

4. Does the concept of the Five-Year Marriage make traditional marriage seem old-fashioned?

That depends on who you are. It is for some people and isn't for others. The Five-Year Marriage isn't for everyone. Like anything else, some people like traditions and want to keep things "as is." Meanwhile, others enthusiastically embrace a new way, like the Five-Year Marriage, especially when it's clear the old way isn't working.

It's reminds me of when the Catholic Church decided to discontinue using Latin as the standard language for its main religious service, the Mass. In the 1960s, when the Pope Paul VI decided to do away with the centuries-old tradition of saying the Mass in Latin, it shocked the faithful. The innovation of saying Mass in a country's mother tongue flipped the Catholic Church on its ear for a few years. And there were other changes, including the priest facing the parishioners, more modern religious songs, and even (heaven forbid) guitar music instead of the traditional organ music.

For many devote Catholics, the changes created a crisis of faith. Some of the faithful, who loved Latin Mass and organ music, were outraged.

At the same time, many found a whole new meaning in their faith. The updating of the Mass made their religion more personal and more real. As a result, they were no longer "Christmas and Easter" Catholics. Instead, they felt more in touch and closer to their religion. They practiced their religion more faithfully.

Still, for many years, a large number of churches continued to offer one Mass in the traditional Latin. Some still do, but only for specially-timed masses.

It's very similar with the Five-Year Marriage. Some people will think of a partnership marriage with a contract attached as almost-heresy. They will hate it and rally against it. Those couples will choose traditional marriage for themselves.

Alternatively, many couples will see the Five-Year Marriage as a better choice and a viable option. That couple is the one interested in creating an equal partnership and making their marriage the centerpiece of their life. The Five-Year Marriage couple will find special meaning in marriage, distinct from that of the traditional couple.

Neither one has to be considered better or worse. Each couple needs to choose the type of marriage that will work best for them and the life they want to live together.

5. Is the Five-Year Marriage legal?

The short answer is "yes" because you get a traditional license, the one that's legal in your state or country. In time, the "forever" marriage license may be a thing of the past, but it isn't now. As of today, if you want to be married legally, you have to do what your local laws require.

If that concerns you, that is, makes you question the advantage of having a five-year commitment, consider this: Couples who cohabitate often say something like, "We don't need a piece of paper to prove our love and commitment." They are correct.

It isn't different with your Five-Year Marriage. A piece of paper (your marriage license) cannot define the constructs of your marriage. That's *your* job. *YOU* define what it means to be married, what it means to live with each other, what a successful marriage is *for you*.

Of course, until the laws change, if you decide to end your relationship after five years, you would get a traditional divorce. If you do, hopefully, you worked out the terms of that divorce in advance of each Five-Year Marriage. In that way, you can end the marriage without acrimony.

6. What if I get pushback from my family or my rabbi/priest/minister? Like, what if my family questions the seriousness of my commitment (for five years).

That's a tough one.

When Joseph and I were married the first time, we didn't broadcast our intention to everyone. So, from the people who *did* know, the only pushback we got was in the form of the question, "But you're going to get a regular marriage license, right?" Since Joseph and I were doing our marriage with a legal tradition that people understood, nobody much cared if we said it was for five years or forever.

However, with each marriage, more people took our Five-Year Marriage more seriously. While their support seemed to legitimize or validate our idea *for them*, it had nothing to do with Joseph and me. Their endorsement didn't change what went on between us from the beginning. We felt our idea was, for us, valid all along.

Still, the Five-Year Marriage is new, unusual, and mostly untried. So if you and your partner are early adopters of the Five-Year Marriage, you will be in the vanguard, true pioneers. I may be the creator, and Joseph and I blazed the trail. But you will be the ones to pave the way, that is, to make it more acceptable to others. So, as with anyone who does something that is avant-garde, some people will love it and support you while others won't.

When you decide to create your own Five-Year Marriage, you have several options when it comes to others:

- Tell your family and get their feelings about it. If they resist, find out why and explain your feelings and reasons for shifting the marriage paradigm. Or...
- Discuss it with only your closet friends. Or...
- Don't discuss it with anyone else (it isn't anyone else's business). Do you think people who have other kinds of unusual marital agreements share those with others? Most of the time, they don't.

One other option: Join a group made up of other Five-Year Marriage couples. You can join Joseph and me in a workshop or online meeting. I recommend doing this because we can help you navigate the road. See FiveYearMarriage.com for more information.

7. What if my family refuses to come to the wedding (or refuses to pay for it) because it's a Five-Year Marriage?

    Most parents will tell you, on the day of their child's wedding, they believed they were attending a wedding that was the beginning of a "forever" marriage. They doubted their child's marriage would end in divorce.

    That probably won't change.

    However, there's something about a child getting married that makes a parent feel like their parental job is complete. Also, it's a party and something fun for them to look forward to, a chance to get a family together for something good. And you can't underestimate your parents' interest in becoming grandparents. If they don't already have grandchildren, your marriage is one step closer to becoming grandparents.

    Yet, as the daughter of a wedding photographer, I saw hundreds of pictures from a lot of weddings, some plain and some fabulous. A year or two or three later, my father would run into a bride or groom whose wedding he photographed and find out the couple had broken up. In fact, to my great surprise, several marriages even broke up before the couple picked up their finished wedding album.

    With that in mind, if you are choosing a Five-Year Marriage, how is it anyone's business if you are getting married traditionally or for five years?

8. What if my family refuses to come to the wedding or my rabbi/priest/minister won't perform the wedding?

    Presuming you are getting a traditional marriage license, there should not be a problem. The only glitch is if you decide to include Five-Year Marriage language in your wedding ceremony or wedding vows. Your rabbi/priest/minister might not want to do the ceremony in that way.

If that is the case, you can bring in a non-denominational officiant to perform the ceremony and ask your rabbi/priest/minister to do a special blessing at the end of the ceremony. Or have your rabbi/priest/minister perform the ceremony and ask the non-denominational officiant to perform the vows part of the ceremony.

NOTE: Joseph and I have had six weddings. Except for avoiding the use of phrases like "till death do you part," we haven't used specific "Five-Year Marriage" language in any wedding ceremony.

9. The Five-Year Marriage is such a new idea. If I got married this way, how do I know I'm doing the right thing?

You don't. Honestly, I don't know if anyone ever knows *anything* for sure, let alone that they're doing the right thing about marriage and the choice of marriage partner. You and your prospective partner want to make the best decision you can, based on the information you have. The "based on the information you have" part is the catch-22. When you're "in love" you are more likely to gloss over some things that you should pay attention to and forgive something that maybe you shouldn't. Your available information is colored by emotion and physical attraction.

That one problem is a big one.

The other "based on the information you have" problem – and it's typical in traditional marriages – is that couples aren't really sure about what they want or what's most important to them. They both come to the relationship with pre-conceived ideas about marriage and marital relationships. Traditional marriages presume that each spouse sees marriage the same way. As discussed in a previous chapter, in reality, they seldom do. Too often ideas about what people want in a marriage are worlds apart, but they aren't discussed. That's a recipe for trouble.

Those are two reasons for why the three *"Five-Year Marriage: The Basics"* chapters (The *Five-Year Marriage Partner*, *The Beginnings*, and *The Nitty Gritty*) are so intense. Those chapters are designed to help you get more and better information, not only about your partner, but about you too. You can figure out and verbalize your own needs and wants before discussing things with your partner.

When you *know* what *you* want and get clear about it in your own mind, you'll picture your purpose in the relationship. You'll go into your marriage meetings with definiteness of purpose and the confidence of clarity. You'll be better at asking for what you want, need and expect in the relationship. In addition, you are both less inclined to settle for what you don't want. That combination is likely to get you more of what makes you happy in the relationship.

One thing is for sure: If you don't know what you want, you will definitely *not* get it. If you are vague, less assertive, or less communicative than your partner, you'll be on the losing end of every discussion. If you are so "in love" that you'll agree to whatever your partner wants, that's not good either. While both of those behaviors will almost surely change by the end of five years, if that's how you are now, I recommend that you talk to a coach, marriage counselor or a mediator. Or, if you need help figuring out the money matters or childcare, connect with an attorney.

One of the beauties of the Five-Year Marriage is that you and your spouse will have a written contract or agreement, predicated on your one-on-one conversations. Still, if you make an agreement that doesn't serve you in *this* Five-Year Marriage, remember that you aren't stuck. You can change it. Keep track and develop new agreements for your next Five-Year Marriage contract.

10. Do the agreements I make in a Five-Year Marriage contract (like, for example, about taking care of children) have any legal standing?

Morally and ethically, they have **great** standing. You are thinking about your children and, no matter what happens between couples, the children should be given proper parental consideration.

However, legally-speaking, your Five-Year Marriage contract may or may not stand up in a court of law. The answer to this question depends on the laws in your state, province, or country. Get legal assistance for the best answer to this question.

11. What happens if something changes dramatically, like one of the partners suffers a disabling injury and can't keep the commitments s/he made when they first wrote the contract?

I'm asked this question a lot – and more by older couples than younger ones. So the answer tends to depend on the reason someone is asking.

If you want to know what happens if one partner has a problem with substance abuse or domestic violence, the most sensible thing is to talk about those issues in advance and include the remedies or outcomes in your Five-Year Marriage contract.

What if one partner loses a job and can't find another one – or, doesn't feel like looking for a job and it becomes a burden to the relationship? Or perhaps that loss (or another kind of loss) leads to debilitating depression that impacts your relationship. Another possibility is that one spouse is diagnosed with an illness or has experienced a military or other type of trauma and suffers from Post-traumatic stress disorder (PTSD).

Life is going to happen and you can't know in advance what tough stuff you will have to handle. There isn't a good agreement anyone can make about those difficult life events.

The one thing you and your partner can agree on in advance is this: If something happens and one or both of you are having difficulty dealing with it (like the death of a child), the person who is in need will agree to get outside help. And the other partner will support him/her as appropriate, including being part of the therapy process.

However, very often, when older couples ask that question, they are thinking about someone suffering a disabling disease, like Alzheimer's. The questions aren't generally about whether to stay together or not. Instead, questions are about end-of-life care preferences. Or, if the couple has children from a previous marriage, they want to know about finances and inheritances.

Those are things you *must* talk about in advance.

For health issues, you can get an end-of-life agreement (Advance Directive/Living Will/Power of Attorney). Then talk about your preferences with each other and let your children know your wishes.

Sometimes, as a financial necessity, an older couple may agree to divorce but stay together. This is never an easy decision and something you must talk to an attorney about so you know your options. [29]

The important thing is to talk about it…even when you don't want to face the possibility that something like that can happen.

12. You always use the words spouse or partner, never husband or wife. Why?

The words "husband" and "wife" aren't part of my personal marriage vocabulary.

Even before the idea for the Five-Year Marriage came to me, I decided that I didn't want to be a "wife." My reason was because I didn't like the connotation commonly given to "wife." It was the result of the many times I sat with another woman, or in a group of women, having conversations about how much we were doing and how busy we were. Often the married women's complaints included being overwhelmed by too many household responsibilities. More than once in those groups, one woman would come to a seemingly logical conclusion to the dilemma and say, "What I need is a wife!" We would all laugh, shaking our heads in agreement.

As I got older, I stopped thinking it was funny.

When a woman talked about something she was doing, I would think, "How dare the world presume that certain responsibilities are automatically a wife's responsibility. If she's a fifty-fifty partner, why does she get stuck with all the obsequious tasks and secretarial responsibilities, from doing laundry to sending all the thank-you notes? Are husbands that stupid or lazy?"

More and more I resented the universally understood expectations put on "the wife" in the relationship. I questioned why "the wife" always took on the roles of things like organizing the couple's social life, overseeing childcare, inviting guests, sending birthday cards, and a plethora of other niceties that simply added to the workload of a woman. That might have made sense for earlier generations, when women were usually stay-at-home moms and household responsibilities were the domain of women.

However, in today's world, more and more women work outside the home, in full-time jobs, and earning a healthy income. They have the same long hours and corporate stress as their spouse. The only fair solution is for the responsibilities that were typically performed solely by a woman in the olden days should now be shared equally by both partners.

The more I saw, the clearer I was about not wanting to be a "wife." However, I knew I wanted a title that I would be happy with and honor, where the word set the stage for the equality I wanted. The most logical gender-neutral word was *spouse*.

Then I wondered, "If I changed the terminology, would that change the behavior?" If I wasn't a *wife* and my man wasn't a *husband*, but if we were both spouses, would we behave differently and would that lend itself to greater equality? I didn't know, but it was worth considering.

Joseph agreed. We wouldn't be "husband" or "wife" but spouses.

However, when we began our first Five-Year Marriage, other people didn't seem to get the message. Joseph especially didn't find it easy, particularly when someone snickered when he said it.

Oddly, I discovered that some people don't even know the word *spouse*. That's less true today than it was twenty or thirty years ago, but I still sometimes get blank stares when I talk about my spouse instead of my husband.

That issue also comes up when talking to some nonagenarians. If I say "spouse" and the listener gets confused, I'll use the "husband" or "wife" words. But it's a rarity.

Also, in the last decade or so, with same-sex marriages becoming more accepted in the culture, people seem to be more comfortable with using spouse to describe a partner (though, interestingly, not necessarily in the LGBTQ community).

Also, in The Five-Year Marriage, I use *partner* as a reminder that you two are creating a partnership. I also use the words "spouse" and "partner" interchangeably. In my life and in real world conversation, *I* use *spouse* (and sometimes "sweetie").

For your purposes, use the word that most enables you to see your relationship as a joint venture.

13. Isn't all the "contracting" talk sort of cold? Like, doesn't all that detail about responsibilities feel like a job with contractual obligations? How do you have love together when everything is a duty?

> First of all, there's nothing cold about all the work you're doing. Getting to agreement is intense and emotional. It's not the same kind of intense as your sex life or as emotional as those *feelings* of love you have. It's the practical side of love.

> After all, you aren't going to do all that hard work with someone you don't love and don't want to be with, *are you*? The whole point of doing all the work is *because* you love and *want* to be together. All the "contracting" is a type of protection for your relationship.

> The seed is love. The Five-Year Marriage encourages that seed grow into a mighty tree.

> Secondly, if you are marrying someone, you *do* have obligations. Even if you are single, you have obligations. You have bills, a mortgage, etc. Do you like your internet or cable service less because you signed a contract? No! You may have some complaints about the service, but you love what it gives you.

> It's the same thing with your Five-Year Marriage contract. When you know what you're supposed to do and what you can expect the other person in the relationship to do (and you both live up to your agreements), it's more likely to create a feeling of safety. Safety, like trust, lends itself to greater intimacy.

> One more thing about this: Have you ever read a contract and realized you don't like what it says? What did you do? Most likely you said "no" and walked away.

> You have the same option with the Five-Year Marriage contract, and you can walk away now – before you even get to

the wedding. In fact, if you aren't feeling good about creating contractual obligations with your sweetie, and committing to them, maybe walking away now is the best thing to do *for both of you.*

14. I think that a Five-Year Marriage wouldn't feel stable. I mean, if we're going to break up in a couple years, why bother?

> The Five-Year Marriage doesn't presume that you will breakup any more than a traditional marriage presumes you will stay together. What it does do is put a frame around your marriage so that your marriage has context within a specific time period (vs. an open-ended "forever").

> The purpose of the Five-Year Marriage isn't to facilitate a break up. With your Five-Year Marriage, you are acknowledging that people change and life changes and that your marriage is willing to flex to the needs of its partners. I think it honors each partner more than a traditional marriage.

> When partners honor each other the best they can, they build trust. Trust is one of the glues that hold people together.

15. I've never been good at negotiations. What do I do about that?

> First of all, what do you think a marital negotiation is? If you think it's about power, being cutthroat or figuring out how to "cut your best deal," or having your way, you're missing the point.

> Negotiation in marriage is give-and-take toward a common goal. It's mutual and reciprocal. That means that one person isn't doing all the giving while the other is doing all the taking. It means that both of you are cooperating with each other to give each other the most of what s/he wants.

> Of course, in the real world, it's easy for the events and challenges of life to create shifts. Even though you have shared goals, sometimes one partner will need more than the other and

vice versa. The scales will tip to favor one partner. If you aren't paying attention, or not speaking up, that tipping can become a pattern instead of a deviation.

That's why having regular Family Meetings is important to your Five-Year Marriage. You'll find that sometimes the whole meeting – or maybe more than one meeting – is all about rebalancing those scales.

Admittedly, sometimes you have to say the same thing *many* times, in a variety of ways, before s/he gets your point. But s/he will *never* get the point if all you do is complain, feel sorry for yourself, whine, or become passive aggressive and let resentment take over.

However, you *can't* say, "I'm not good at negotiations" and let that become an acceptable excuse. It isn't. If you aren't speaking up (that is, before you blow up), *shame on you!* It's *your responsibility*, as a good partner, to express yourself clearly and definitively.

In fact, the most important thing you need to have in the Five-Year Marriage may not be love. Maybe it isn't even communication (though little can mitigate the need for strong communication). Maybe the one thing that can supersede even your communication skills could be *the belief, the understanding, that you are partners who will go farther - faster - when you go together.* Remember, you are traveling together because you:

- Share values.
- Know each other's expectations and feel you are in tune with them (without becoming someone you aren't).
- Have a common destination that you will both love (e.g., a certain lifestyle, having a family, etc.).
- Have shared goals that challenge both of you to be the best you can be.

When you see your relationship through that lens, both of you will see it's in *both* your best interests to be on the same page in your relationship. It also means that you will strive to accommodate each other's needs because that helps both of you be your best self in the relationship.

That's why you *must* speak up. If you aren't good at negotiations, get some help doing it. Sometimes reading a book and then practicing with friends will help you build your skills.

At the same time, don't expect other people to change overnight. Or be a mind-reader.

I've heard it so many times: "S/he should have known…" or "I would have hoped that s/he would have cared enough…" That kind of thinking never ends well. You can't rely on your partner to read your mind. S/he is busy and s/he is not a psychic. S/he doesn't mean to be selfish, uncaring, and self-absorbed (unless, of course, you married a narcissist…and if you were working the three *"Five-Year Marriage Basics"* chapters you probably found that out – and should have walked away).

And you can't expect that your partner is oh-so-generous that s/he will easily shift out of a long-standing and comfortable behavior into a new one.

Remember, you are both busy. And becoming distracted is as easy as breathing. It happens to the best of us and sometimes at the most inopportune moments. As a result, it's really easy to forget what you said you would/would not do. Sometimes your partner will get so distracted that s/he needs the proverbial two-by-four between the eyes so s/he will pay attention.

Sometimes the distracted person will be you.

When you fall short (and you will sometimes), you admit it, regroup, and do better. When your partner falls short, you call it out, honestly share your feelings, and await something better – but expect progress, not perfection.

Again, that's what the Family Meeting addresses.

16. Do I have to compromise on everything?

First, understand what it means to *compromise*. According to the Cambridge Dictionary, "a compromise is an agreement between two sides who have different opinions, in which each side gives up something it had wanted."

What's in your background that makes you think compromise is the natural or obligatory course in a marriage partnership?

I don't think it has to be. In fact, I hate the idea of compromise. To me, compromise means a concession. It means settling for something I don't want.

I believe the Five-Year Marriage is designed to hold back compromise.

For example, clarity circumvents compromise. If you are clear about what you want and are willing to say it (and keep saying it), you are less likely to have to compromise.

If you aren't clear about your needs and wants, you won't get it.

If you say what you want and, when you don't get it, let your own requests be ignored and slide into oblivion, you're compromising.

In the Five-Year Marriage, you aren't looking for some fairy tale life – that is, *you're* perfect and always right, and *s/he* is flawed and always wrong. Presuming you intend to live in the real world, during your Five-Year Marriage you are both going to give and take. Sometimes you are doing the giving and other times you are doing the taking. But, if it's healthy, it cannot always be one way.

In the end, the Five-Year Marriage can facilitate the process of getting what you want, instead of forcing you to settle for whatever you can get.

17. I love the Five-Year Marriage idea but my boyfriend hates this idea. He says he doesn't want all our "everything" spelled out. He feels like "the nuns" are going to be watching. What do I tell him?

So you're having your first power struggle!

Well, you can tell him there are no "nuns" to watch him. After he stops laughing, you can ask him what that "nuns" thing means to him. Does it mean that he will feel compelled to stick to his agreements? Is it accountability that he hates? That's something good to know going into any relationship. It's also a good reason to see a marriage counselor.

Maybe he has responsibility issues. It could be that he doesn't want to have anything spelled out in case he doesn't follow through on the commitment.

The Five-Year Marriage really helps you understand quickly that talk is cheap and actions speak louder than words.

Of course your boyfriend's feelings may have nothing to do with accountability or responsibility.

One of the reasons that you talk about your agreements, get them in writing, and review them regularly is because human nature lends itself to not following through on the things you say you're going to do, especially if you don't think you'll be held accountable.

If he wants a traditional marriage and you don't, that's a problem. I suggest you go through *The Beginnings* chapter with him and find out what you both really want in a marriage. You may or may not be on the same page about what marriage means to you, the kind of marriage you want, your goals and values, and what you want out of marriage.

Knowing that information could be eye-opening for both of you. You may need to step back and think about who you are and who he is. You may want to rethink the whole marriage idea, *at least with him.*

Based on the question, I'm referring to the boyfriend who doesn't want a Five-Year Marriage. However, it could easily be the woman who isn't interested. In that case, you want to ask similar questions and get clarity around her reasons.

The decision about whether to have a Five-Year Marriage isn't the same as which band or DJ you want to play at your wedding or where you're going to live. It's much more important. And it's a decision that will be way more long-lasting than who you choose for your wedding music.

18. As the Five-Year Marriage continues, will the romance and commitment continue?

That's a good question. The answer is "maybe."

First, let's talk about the commitment part.

The Oxford Dictionary says commitment is "the state or quality of being dedicated to a cause" or "a pledge or undertaking" or "an engagement or obligation that restricts freedom of action." However, I personally prefer The Urban Dictionary definition, which says *commitment* means "sticking with something long after the mood you have said it in has left you." That sounds more like the Five-Year Marriage kind of commitment.

The Five-Year Marriage is a commitment for five years. That means you dedicate yourself to the partnership you create for five years. Thinking of that in terms of the Oxford Dictionary, it means that you and your partner choose what you're committing to for five years. You talk about everything from your bigger picture (values, expectations and goals) to the more mundane (everyday tasks).

For example, if you commit to being faithful, you agree not to have an affair. If you commit to having dedicated couple time or Family Meeting, that *could mean*, from time to time, passing on a golf game, or a night out with your girls or guys. It doesn't have to be that, *but it might* if you two can't otherwise find time for each other.

Once you agree, then you (1) pledge to stick to those terms for five years and (2) agree to fully *dedicate yourselves* to your chosen responsibilities to each other – for five years. You aren't stuck with these commitments *forever*, but you *are* committed to them for five years. If you decide to get married again, you can add, delete, or change the commitments.

Now, the more complicated part of the question: romance. At *this* point in *your* life, what *is* romance *to you*?

The Urban Dictionary defines romance as:
> "…doing something special or unexpected for someone you love, even though you don't have to. Romance isn't a greeting card, it isn't Valentine's Day, it isn't a box of chocolates, and it certainly isn't a dozen roses (unless you like that sort of thing). Real romance is not what modern society has been taught to think it is. Real romance isn't manufactured. It is completely individual. Romance is for showing the person you love that you're thinking about them. It shouldn't feel forced. There are no limits to romance; it can be shown by a handwritten note, by going for a walk, or even by making someone a sandwich. Romance is something simple and sweet that reminds your partner why they fell in love with you in the first place."

As such, expressions of romance are likely to change over time.

When you were first together, romance might have been getting flowers from your sweetie or having hotel sex. In those early days, you needed that to show that you two were in sync and s/he loved you.

The longer you are together, you are very likely to think and feel differently about what constitutes romance. You may find other things to be more appropriate romantic symbols of your love. The old hearts and flowers thing is likely to give way to more substantive signs of romance.

Many new mothers say that watching their spouse get up in the middle of the night to change a crying baby so she can get some sleep is the most romantic thing their spouse could do. Guys say that it's romantic when she puts her arms around him for no reason or she tells him how important he is to her or how she loves it when he makes her laugh.

Romance could also be coming home from a long day at work, thinking you have to cook dinner – and your partner did it already. All you have to do it sit down and eat; that's *very* romantic.

Not that the flowers or jewelry (or other "buys") aren't good or appreciated. They are. It's just that, in the beginning, that's *all* you have, all you know *how* to do, so it works.

When you are further down the marital road, if you are in a loving relationship, flowers and candy just don't carry the same emotional weight as they did when you were newly together.

In fact, for some couples, doing those same things could have the opposite effect. For example, if you're treating me like crap or you're having an affair, then sending me flowers or buying me candy is hurtful (at best); it causes wounded and bitter feelings.

In my house, the motto is "Talk is cheap and actions speak louder than words." My opinion is that anybody can throw money at something, like candy and flowers, or buy some necklace on sale at the local jewelers. That's not necessarily romance.

That's one of the reasons you put together a "Ten Things That Make Me Feel Special" list. If your sweetie cares enough to remember the list, check it, and then do one thing that is on it, *isn't that pretty romantic?*

Here's a special note just to you guys: Your girlfriend or spouse wants to know that ***she's special to you***. She still wants you to think of her as "your girlfriend" even when you've been married for a lifetime. When you treat her like she's just another one of the guys, or like the store clerk (and maybe not even as friendly), she feels common, like the wrapping paper on your favorite guilty pleasure chocolate. She doesn't want to feel like the wrapping paper, she wants to feel like the chocolate. Specifically, she wants to know that you are at least as excited about her as you are for that two-dollar piece of candy.

Keep that idea in mind as you look over her "Ten Things" list and, once a month, do one of those things. It won't matter to her that you took it from the list. It will matter to her that you paid enough attention to look at the list and plan something.

What's romance to you? S/he might need a roadmap. Make it easy for your spouse to be romantic by keeping your "what makes me feel special" list up to date. Also, it helps, when s/he does something romantic, say how much you liked it and exactly why you thought it was romantic. Reinforcement matters.

Personally, to me, the candy and flowers thing is trite. I like them, but they haven't been a symbol of romance to me since Joseph and I were dating. What is romantic is that we do Family Meetings. They aren't easy, but they matter, and they make me feel like Joseph cares about me enough to make our discourses a priority in both our lives. That's a solid demonstration of romance to me.

Romance is also when we dance and Joseph holds me close, holds my hand when we walk someplace, or watches out for me when we're in a crowd (even though I know I'm fully capable of watching out for myself).

One night, at the end of vacation, Joseph and I were in Newburyport Massachusetts. While there, we met a group of people at the Thirsty Whale bar. We were all professional people at a Friday Happy Hour. We were talking business and life and I was having a great time. Unfortunately, I wasn't paying attention to how much I was drinking. I didn't realize I was getting pretty toasted. Fortunately, Joseph did. If I had stayed, I would have gotten really drunk. Fortunately, Joseph got me out of the bar before I embarrassed myself and back to the hotel before anything "bad" happened.

I have wonderful memories of the people I met at the Thirsty Whale that night...and, thanks to Joseph, I was out of there before I did something that would have put a cloud on that memory. That's romance to me.

Also, almost every night Joseph and I are together, he makes me a cup of tea. It seems like a dumb little thing, but when he asks me if I'll join him (in our kitchen) for a cup of tea, I like it. Then, as if he thinks I'll turn him down, he "entices" me into saying "yes" with an "I'm buying." That's the kind of romance that a box of calorie-laden chocolates or already dying flowers could never do for me.

19. Do you actually do the things you're telling other people to do?

Yes! Most of what I've written came to me, and to Joseph and me, through trial and error.

Yes, Joseph and I *do* re-contract at the end of a marriage. Yes, we have Family Meetings, though we don't seem to need as many meetings as we did before. We usually do them when something is going on (like something in business or a personal crisis) and our lives get too busy to keep up with certain responsibilities. Yes, we practice getting better at our communication skills. Yes, we make the effort to be polite.

Joseph and I do the things I've suggested to you. We do them even when it's convenient to forget about them.

We are still learning how to live together – in *this* Five-year Marriage.

Still, Joseph and I aren't perfect people and we don't always do it right. We hurt each other's feelings. We get off track. Or stuff happens when we're out with friends. Sometimes we have an all-out argument. It's normal living-together stuff.

The difference between us and a traditionally married couple is that we have the blueprint in place, and a pattern of following the blueprint. So when things get wonky, we know what to do to get back on track. It works for us.

I believe it will work for you too. That's why I'm sharing everything with you.

Now you have the blueprint too!

20. You don't have children. How do you think you would have handled this with children in your Five-Year Marriage?

The one thing I believe I would do, if I had children, is gradually bring them into the Family Meeting debates.

From my years as a school teacher and my years as an office and department manager, I learned that it's up to the head of the group to set the tone. And, of course, children learn what they live.

Also, in 1997, the late Stephen Covey wrote a wonderful book called the *Seven Habits of Highly Effective Families.* Joseph and I were already entrenched in our pattern for Family Meetings, but we devoured the audio of that book while on a road trip.

Covey talked about having a family mission statement and doing other things that Joseph and I were already doing. However, Covey's ideas supplied us with a couple tweaks to our process.

Through Covey's book I could envision how it would be to incorporate kids into the mix of the Five-Year Marriage. I recognized that children would become part of a democratic process, of sorts, and watch a healthy dose of disagreement and problem solving while experiencing respect for differing opinions.

So, in a Five-Year Marriage *with children*, I would still have Family Meetings but invite the children (but not to every meeting). However, when the meeting includes the children, I would have a private meeting first, just with Joseph. That's so we could get on the same page and provide effective leadership within our family. Then I would follow that up with a monthly or weekly meeting with the children during which they could participate in venting their frustrations as well as accepting responsibilities for household activities.

The Family Meeting begins a positive pattern for communication that the children can take into their adult relationships.

21. When you were engaged the first time, did you have any inkling that the relationship wasn't right?

This interesting question was asked during the very first radio interview I gave about the Five-Year Marriage. The answer is "yes" but until that moment on the air, I'd totally forgotten something that happened about a week or so before I ended that engagement.

You already know, from earlier in this book, that I was the quintessential Italian "good girl" in my family. Everything in my background had me on a path to marriage and children. In addition, everyone I knew was already married or getting married. There were a lot of weddings where I got the "When are you getting married?" question – and I was tired of hearing it. I *really* wanted to be on the "marriage track" and I got engaged. I really thought I was ready. Until…

After a typically good Friday night date in early September, I went home to bed. I slept soundly, until very early in the morning when I had an alarming dream. To this very day I can remember it like I dreamed it this morning.
In the special style of dream-movies, I saw myself showing off my very lovely diamond ring. What was odd was that the diamond looked *very* big, way out of proportion to my hand.

Suddenly, and much to my surprise, I watched some unknown person position a chisel over the diamond, dead center. Then, with a hammer, someone hit the head of the chisel and shattered the diamond into a million pieces.

As you might expect, I woke up with a start. As I slowly tried piecing together what had just happened, I felt very disturbed, even panicky, and sick to my stomach. I didn't know what it meant, but one thing I knew for sure, someone decimating the diamond of my engagement ring wasn't a good sign.

Of course, I didn't know then that the dream was a premonition. In fact, if I'd been given that dream as an omen, a forewarning, I ignored the warning because I didn't want to believe it. So I did what so many brides-to-be do. I brushed it off. At least I tried. The feeling kept coming back to me, several times a day. Doggedly, I kept ignoring it.

It was a couple weeks later, when (as described early in this book) Marie relayed Tom's concerns about Jimmy to me. I wanted to believe what Jimmy was just spouting guy-swagger and push my troubled thoughts aside.

I might have done that *except* for the dream with the smashed diamond. It kept playing and playing in the back of my head.

Honestly, I didn't want to end my engagement and my "Sadie-Sadie-Married-Lady" dream. For a long time, I was devastated by it. Still, it was a turning point in my life.

Looking back, I believe I would have been terribly unhappy. I doubt I would have stayed married. In fact, after later revelations, I'm sure – at least I hope – I would have divorced him.

Still, by the time I would have pulled myself together enough to make the divorce decision, I'm pretty sure I would have been the single mother of two or three kids. If I had, my challenges would have been like those facing most single mothers.

I doubt I would have found my own voice, or come into my own power, or fulfilled my purpose in life. Would I even think about shaping those challenges into personal victories? Or, would I have been a victim of my circumstances?

I hope I would have done a stellar job pulling myself out of a bad marriage and rising to the top. Then maybe some woman would have written my story, the way I wrote about the amazing women in my first book, *Victorious Woman: Shaping Life's Challenges into Personal Victories*.

Either way, my life would have been very, very different than the life I have.

Instead, during those first years after the broken engagement, I spent a lot of time in serious soul-searching followed by a lot of growth and self-development. I designed my life in a very distinct way from the good girl lifestyle in which I'd been raised.

I'm a better woman because of it.

Of course, I wonder… if I was a divorced single mom, would I ever have met Joseph? Then I wonder…without him, as my partner, would I have created the Five-Year Marriage? I'll never know.

Over the years many women have told me that "something" happened during their courtship or engagement. They chose to ignore it, too, and regretted it later. I wondered if my "premonition" was some kind of psychic preparation for what I needed to do. Would I have taken the steps I did if I wasn't psychically prepared? I don't think so.

So I'm sharing this experience with you. If you are reading this and you have any kind of premonition about the person you're thinking of marrying, *pay attention*. Refuse to be lulled into ignoring those feelings. I want you to know that my decision to end that relationship was hard, but was a blessing in disguise.

Don't worry about what other people might say, or if somebody is angry with you (like my father was with me) or is disappointed. Following your intuition, and your mind instead of your heart, could mean ending a bad or unhealthy relationship that serves no one and only contributes to the sadness of the world.

At the same time, it could mean that, once you pick up the pieces, you learn and grow stronger. Sometimes the thing that seems like the worst thing that could have happened turns out to be the very best.

Afterword

To love someone deeply gives you strength.
Being loved by someone deeply gives you courage.
Lao Tzu, Chinese Philosopher

I believe you have choices. Most of the time, you can choose what you want for a lifestyle, career, place to live, and more.

With those choices (and even the non-choices) come challenges.

In addition, you don't know what interesting thing will come your way. You can have a sudden financial or health challenge, or someone dies, and you are having more difficulty dealing with it than you expected. That's all part of life. However, even when something bad happens, you can choose your attitude about it. That's true about every single thing that happens in your life.

You can't control everything that comes your way. Thinking that you *can* is a setup for constant frustration and disappointment.

It's no different with the Five-Year Marriage.

However, what you *can* do is stay on top of the things that *are* in your control. And, in your Five-Year Marriage, you and your spouse have that opportunity. You choose each other, of course. From then on, throughout your Five-Year Marriage, you'll make choices and decisions as partners.

Together you two shape your experiences into your shared and personal victories.

When you choose the Five-Year Marriage, you are choosing to build the life you were meant to live – with trust, intimacy, and joy – five years at a time.

And, as that strong woman or man, and as that robust couple, you contribute to the joy and positive energy of your family, your friends, and the world.

It's all in your hands – the good, the bad, the ugly.

What do you want?

Are you willing to take the risk implied in the Five-Year Marriage?

Do you think it's more or less risk than a traditional marriage?

Are you willing to do the work of a Five-Year Marriage?

The ball is in your court, the canvas is blank…choose whatever phrase you like. It's your life and…

You get to choose…

One Last Thing...

Since first coming up with the Five-Year Marriage idea in 1988, Joseph has been my "lab partner" in this fascinating experiment. So, as I wrote the first draft, chapter by chapter, I asked for his feedback.

After several edits, and when the book was just about ready to go to print, I wanted us to "experience" the book together - *the way you are doing*. So Joseph and I read each chapter aloud over a three-week period. After each chapter, we'd talk a little about what I'd written.

Of course, we were reminded of the details of our relationship, the good times, the bad ones and the tough stuff. We were able to recall where we were or what was going on when we talked about some of *The Beginnings* or *The Nitty Gritty* questions or something else. Overall, we were satisfied with what we shared with you.

I guess Joseph was thinking about everything because, for couple weeks afterward, he would bring something up about our Five-Year Marriage. Sometimes it was a shared story that reminded him of another part of our relationship. Other times he commented on a question or set of questions.

One night we walked into our little town of West Chester for dinner. The subject of the book came up. We talked about it and then Joseph said, "You know, I knew this was going to be a good book. But it's even better than I thought. It tells people all the important stuff they need to know."

To tell you that I was touched would be an understatement. Knowing that Joseph endorsed what I wrote was good. But his comments revealed to me that he is as invested in communicating with you the workings of this Five-Year Marriage experiment as much as I am.

Joseph and I believe in the Five-Year Marriage. Yes, we know it isn't for everyone, *but it could be for you.*

If it is, know that Joseph and I are thinking about you. We picture you having the tough conversations. We visualize you getting better and better at communicating with each other and getting stronger together. We see your children learning valuable life lessons that they will take with them into their adult lives and adult relationships. We envision many happy Five-Year Marriages for you and see you being filled with the joy of intimacy.

And we're ready to help you. See FiveYearMarriage.com for the blog, classes, and more.

Finally, keep this in mind: If you know the destination and you keep going, even rough roads can take you to wonderful places.

Acknowledgements

My Five-Year Marriage couldn't have happened without my partnership with my spouse, Joseph Eagle. So, naturally, I wanted to make sure he was an active part of everything I wrote. He was a great support and contributed good thoughts and suggestions each time.

However, I really wanted you, the reader, to hear from Joseph himself. So I asked him to write something for each chapter. He readily agreed to do it but I soon understood it was a bigger "ask" than I realized. You see, Joseph doesn't see himself as a writer. So that was hard all by itself. But because Joseph wants every reader to understand how much he believes in the Five-Year Marriage, he stressed about the wording of every thought and opinion he shared with you.

So, while Joseph easily *talks* about the Five-Year Marriage, *writing* the "Joseph's Take" section for each chapter was almost painful for him.

I appreciate what Joseph did. And I look forward to Joseph sharing more with you – *but I can almost guarantee – it'll be in an interview, video or podcast!*

Thank you, Joseph!

When I wrote the first draft of Five-Year Marriage, I didn't do anything with it. In fact, I boxed it up and put it away. In September 2000, author and professor Lisa Jobs asked me to give her Rosemont College Publishing Class a project. I gave them Five-Year Marriage. Lisa's Fall2000 class had discussions, did focus groups, and more. When I returned in December, I was impressed with their work. More importantly, their work was the first of many "nudges" I received to finish Five-Year Marriage. Nice work to Lisa and her class!

When I first talked to author, Hollywood script consultant, and book coach Barbara Schiffman in 2016, it was about having her join me as a guest on my weekly radio show, "The Friday Happy Hour with Annmarie Kelly." After we did the show, I talked to her again. I told her I was stalled in my writing. During that conversation, Barbara told me she saw the Five-Year Marriage in a bigger picture than I did. It was exciting! What she said that day flipped a switch in my head. I got motivated and moving.

Shortly after that conversation with Barbara, I had breakfast with friend Donna Cavanaugh, an author and the publisher at HumorOutcasts Press and Shorehouse Books. Though that breakfast – like all our breakfasts - kept us laughing so much that we made the other restaurant patrons jealous, Donna managed to give me enough encouragement to keep me writing Five-Year Marriage. Along the way, whenever I was panicky about what I was doing, a phone call or email with Donna made a difference. Thanks so much, Donna! See you down the shore!

And the same to you, author, attorney, and humorist Cathy Sikorski. The day when I was online and found your blog was a good day for me! Your knowledge of eldercare issues is priceless, and they've helped my Happy Hour listeners. Last year, when you read an early draft of the "Five-Year Marriage," you told me you loved it. You prodded me to get it going. And you made me laugh in a way that few people can. I'll be seeing you in Manhattan!

My cousin, Maryann Volpe, and my friend, Helen Gallagher, were earlier and also later "readers" of the manuscript. Maryann's work-related talent for catching repeated information was really helpful and Helen asked great questions. Thanks to both of you!

Thanks too to editor Julie Ritzer Ross. She corrected some things, tightened other things up, and made the Five-Year Marriage easier for you to read.

Thanks to all the people who listened to me – for years – about writing the Five-Year Marriage. I know there were times you thought I'd never finish it. I did too! But I'm glad you kept asking me about it.

Also, I can't even name all the people who read portions of the "Five-Year Marriage" and had good comments and encouraged me. Your interest, and sometimes even just your questions, spurred me on to finish my writing. I appreciate each and every one of you!

Finally, thanks to the God and Goddess of love and creativity. You gave me the idea for the Five-Year Marriage and I'm a happier woman because of it. And you kept nudging me along to share it with others so they can be happier and get the most out of their marriages – and their lives, and their children's lives. I'm forever grateful!

RESOURCES

SAMPLE FIVE-YEAR MARRIAGE CONTRACT

Today's Date _____

We, **NAME** and **NAME**, decide the following for this Five-Year Marriage, which starts on **DATE** and ends on **DATE**

Here's why we want to be married (intention):

_____

_____

The reason we're together for this Five-Year Marriage (purpose) is:

_____

_____

The things that matter most to us are (write your top five values – and why they are important):

_____

_____

_____

_____

Here's what we agree to work toward during this Five-Year Marriage (vision and goals):

_____

_____

_____

_____

_____

What we can expect from each other (this can include honestly, fidelity, respect, children, taking care of children, and also things like keeping the house straightened up, having family dinners…things that are important to both of you – and that you two talked about and agreed on in the "Five-Year Marriage Basics" chapters):

_____

_____

_____

_____

Some of the "buzzwords" (common themes) that will remind us of these are:

_____

_____

_____

_____

_____

Our "headlight" conversations are things we can talk about at family meetings, including:

_____

_____

_____

_____

_____

We agree to these and are entering this Five-Year Marriage with love:

_____   _____

Name   Name

FIVE-YEAR MARRIAGE BUILDING BLOCKS

The "Solid Seven" traits you're looking for in the Five-Year Marriage Partner (detailed in Chapter Three)

Emotional Chemistry
Ongoing Dialogue
Dependability
Personal Responsibility
Freedom
Fairness
Mutual Respect

THE GROUND RULES:
See Chapters Four and Five for explanations about each of these:

1. Set a Time for your Family Meeting and make it an appointment
2. Choose a neutral place
3. Have an agenda
4. Slow Down: don't try to squeeze your sharing conversations (and, later, your contracting exchanges) into a single meeting or a single day
5. Make it a conversation
6. Do your homework
7. Be pleasant, patient and open-minded
8. Stay Positive
9. Stay focused
10. Be HONEST
11. Stick to the topic
12. Be respectful of your partner
13. Agree to brainstorm

THE SIX KEYS
(for keeping your Five-Year Marriage up to speed, described in Chapter Six)

1. Mind the Store
2. Follow the Ground Rules
3. Turn the Communication Key
4. Remember Your Purpose
5. Make Magic with Habits
6. Make the Most of Your Family Meetings

BOOKS WORTH READING
FOR FIVE-YEAR MARRIAGE COUPLES

Crucial Conversations: Tools for Talking When the Stakes are High – Kerry Patterson and Joseph Grenny

Crucial Confrontations: Tools for Resolving Broken Promised, Violated Expectations, and Bad Behavior - Kerry Patterson and Joseph Grenny

The Five Love Languages: The Secret to Love that Lasts – Gary Chapman

Passage to Intimacy – Lori Gordon and Jon Frandsen

The Magic of Thinking Big – David Schwartz

The Seven Habits of Highly Effective Families – Stephen Covey

ASSESSMENTS FOR FIVE-YEAR MARRIAGE COUPLES

DiSC Personal Profile – FiveYearMarriage.com

Coping and Stress Profile - FiveYearMarriage.com

FINDING A MARRIAGE COUNSELOR OR
MARITAL MEDIATOR

I think the best way to find a marriage counselor or mediator is to get a referral. When Joseph and I decided to get outside help, our marriage counselor was referred to us by a woman who had two things that were important to Joseph and me. She shared our values and she knew the counselor from having been to him for therapy (versus just knowing him through work or something).

But, if you cannot find a referral, or don't want to ask a friend for one, try these online resources:

American Association of Marriage and Family Therapists: http://www.aamft.org.

American Psychological Association - http://www.apa.org/

Psychology Today Therapists - https://therapists.psychologytoday.com/rms

https://www.mediate.com

CHAPTER NOTES

Chapter Two

[1] Divorce Tables – United States:
http://www.cdc.gov/nchs/nvss/marriage_divorce_tables.htm

[2] Divorce Tables – Europe: http://ec.europa.eu/eurostat/statistics-explained/index.php/Marriage_and_divorce_statistics

[3] Pew Social Trends: http://www.pewsocialtrends.org/2010/11/18/the-decline-of-marriage-and-rise-of-new-families/2/#ii-overview

[4] Marriage and Divorce Chart:
http://www.randalolson.com/2015/06/15/144-years-of-marriage-and-divorce-in-1-chart/

[5] Susan Sarandon Interview:
http://www.telegraph.co.uk/culture/8023313/Im-Still-a-Hippie-Chick-Susan-Sarandon-interview.html

[6] Mexican Marriage:
http://www.cnn.com/2011/10/03/world/americas/mexico-2-year-marriages

[7] http://blogs.abc.net.au/tasmania/files/marriage_contracts_helen_goltz.pdf

[8] Australian Marriage:
http://www.diyfamilylawaustralia.com/Topic/divorce_marriage_less_two_years.html
Also:
http://www.familycourt.gov.au/wps/wcm/connect/fcoaweb/reports-and-publications/publications/separation/have-you-been-married-less-than-two-years

[9] http://www.ehbonline.org/article/S1090-5138(01)00101-5/pdf

[10] http://www.smithsonianmag.com/history/how-american-rich-kids-bought-their-way-into-the-british-elite-4252/?no-ist

[11] http://www.usatoday.com/story/news/nation/2014/04/26/shotgun-weddings-marriage-pregnant/7794029/

[12] http://msmagazine.com/blog/2013/05/28/10-things-that-american-women-could-not-do-before-the-1970s/
Also: http://www.nytimes.com/1983/06/28/style/changing-women-s-names.html

[13] http://www.history.com/topics/world-war-ii/american-women-in-world-war-ii,
Also: https://www.pinterest.com/explore/rosie-riveter/

[14] http://www.nber.org/digest/jan07/w12139.html

[15] http://nationalmarriageproject.org/wordpress/wp-content/uploads/2014/08/NMP-BeforeIDoReport-Final.pdf
Also: http://www.cosmopolitan.com/sex-love/a39366/first-comes-baby-then-comes-marriage/

[16] https://www.cdc.gov/nchs/fastats/marriage-divorce.htm

[17] http://www.huffingtonpost.com/2013/01/18/marriage-research_n_2506980.html

[18] https://www.cdc.gov/nchs/data/hus/2010/022.pdf
Also: https://www.census.gov/population/socdemo/hh-fam/tabMS-2.pdf

People of the Lake: https://www.amazon.com/People-Lake-Mankind-Its-Beginnings/dp/0380455757?tag=skillsyste-20

Chapter Three

[19]https://www.bing.com/videos/search?q=rachel+ray+%2b+rob+lowe
&view=detail&mid=EDFCC049975C30405A94EDFCC049975C304
05A94&FORM=VIRE

[20] http://www.usnews.com/news/slideshows/9-reasons-why-you-should-get-married-for-yourself-and-for-america

[21] http://www.huffingtonpost.com/divorced-moms/10-reasons-people-get-married-when-they-know-better_b_6985040.html

[22] http://www.match.com/magazine/article/13403/Does-Chemistry

[23] http://www.mayoclinic.org/diseases-conditions/narcissistic-personality-disorder/basics/symptoms/con-20025568

[24]https://www.psychologytoday.com/blog/the-mysteries-love/201503/15-kinds-verbal-abuse
Also:
http://www.aamft.org/iMIS15/AAMFT/Content/Consumer_Updates/Domestic_violence.aspx

[25] http://www.wikihow.com/Spot-a-Sociopath

Also:__ https://www.psychologytoday.com/articles/201305/how-spot-sociopath

Chapter Five

[26] https://www.youtube.com/watch?v=vhXutOdZOoE

Also: http://www.eonline.com/news/775387/jon-gosselin-spills-on-what-s-going-on-between-him-kate-and-their-kids-it-s-bad-right-now

[27] http://www.therapyinphiladelphia.com/tips/having-a-conversation-to-assert-your-boundaries

28

http://psychologytoday.tests.psychtests.com/take_test.php?idRegTest =1299

Chapter Eight

29   https://www.forbes.com/sites/feeonlyplanner/2014/08/21/divorce-due-to-medical-bills-sometimes-it-makes-sense/#54d1e12b74b8

A Five-Year Marriage Invitation for You

Dear Smart and Savvy Couple,

Are you interested in becoming a Five-Year Marriage couple? If you are, first, Congratulations!

Want to be part of a research project with other couples who are also choosing the Five-Year Marriage? I'd love for you to join them - and me!!

I'm interested in hearing from couples of all kinds, ages, socio-economic backgrounds, political ideologies, and religions.

It doesn't matter if this is your first marriage or not. If it's your **first Five-Year Marriage**, *I want you to be part of this project.* We'll find out what works best for you and what doesn't, where you are having the most fun, what poses the greatest challenge, and what is the best thing for you about your Five-Year Marriage. And you'll connect with other couples who are also choosing the Five-Year Marriage.

I hope you'll join me and be part of this ground-breaking research!

You can find me at FiveYearMarriage.com/research.

I look forward to working with you, answering your questions, helping you along the way and sharing your joys!

With love,

Annmarie

About Annmarie Kelly

ANNMARIE KELLY has been married six times, each time for five years. She's waited a long time to share the Five-Year Marriage with couples.

While she was working on her own Five-Year Marriage, Annmarie became an award-winning leader, author, corporate trainer, professional speaker, and the host of the Friday Happy Hour. She works with corporations, leadership groups, professional associations, and individuals, encouraging people to *LIVE VICTORIOUSLY – out loud and in living color.*

In 2008, Annmarie founded The Victorious Woman Project, which focuses on inspiration, education and encouragement by providing resources for "starting over" women and leadership skills for women in the workplace. She is also the founder of the Girlfriend Gala, an annual fundraiser which has benefitted the homeless, women in transition, and most recently, non-traditional women college students through the Victorious Woman Scholarship at Neumann University.

Annmarie is the author of two other books, *Victorious Woman! Shaping Life's Challenges into Personal Victories* and *Victory by Design*, as well as many articles on a variety of topics, including: emotional intelligence, goal achievement, behavior-focused performance improvement, mentoring, and life balance. She is a professional member of National Speakers Association and holds an advanced speaker designation (DTM) with Toastmasters International.

Annmarie lives in Chester County, Pennsylvania, with her spouse, Joseph Eagle. She loves taking long walks, traveling, vacationing in Downeast Maine, and enjoying time with her friends.

28481161R00139

Made in the USA
Columbia, SC
13 October 2018